Information Architecture for Information Professionals

CHANDOS
INFORMATION PROFESSIONAL SERIES

Series Editor: Ruth Rikowski
(email: Rikowskigr@aol.com)

Chandos' new series of books are aimed at the busy information professional. They have been specially commissioned to provide the reader with an authoritative view of current thinking. They are designed to provide easy-to-read and (most importantly) practical coverage of topics that are of interest to librarians and other information professionals. If you would like a full listing of current and forthcoming titles, please visit our web site **www.chandospublishing.com** or contact Hannah Grace-Williams on email info@chandospublishing.com or telephone number +44 (0) 1865 884447.

New authors: we are always pleased to receive ideas for new titles; if you would like to write a book for Chandos, please contact Dr Glyn Jones on email gjones@chandospublishing.com or telephone number +44 (0) 1865 884447.

Bulk orders: some organisations buy a number of copies of our books. If you are interested in doing this, we would be pleased to discuss a discount. Please contact Hannah Grace-Williams on email info@chandospublishing.com or telephone number +44 (0) 1865 884447.

Information Architecture for Information Professionals

SUE BATLEY

Chandos Publishing

Oxford · England

Chandos Publishing (Oxford) Limited
Chandos House
5 & 6 Steadys Lane
Stanton Harcourt
Oxford OX29 5RL
UK
Tel: +44 (0) 1865 884447 Fax: +44 (0) 1865 884448
Email: info@chandospublishing.com
www.chandospublishing.com

First published in Great Britain in 2007

ISBN:
978 1 84334 232 8 (paperback)
978 1 84334 233 5 (hardback)
1 84334 232 4 (paperback)
1 84334 233 2 (hardback)

© Sue Batley, 2007

British Library Cataloguing-in-Publication Data.
A catalogue record for this book is available from the British Library.

The Publishers make no representation, express or implied, with regard to the accuracy of the
information contained in this publication and cannot accept any legal responsibility or liability
for any errors or omissions.

The material contained in this publication constitutes general guidelines only and does not
represent to be advice on any particular matter. No reader or purchaser should act on the basis
of material contained in this publication without first taking professional advice appropriate to
their particular circumstances.

Typeset by Domex e-Data Pvt. Ltd.
Printed in the UK and USA.

For my mum and dad

Contents

List of abbreviations		*xi*
List of figures		*xiii*
Preface		*xvii*
About the author		*xix*
1	**Information architecture: an introduction**	**1**
	Information architecture defined	1
	Core concepts	4
	Summary	10
	Further reading	10
	References	11
2	**The preliminaries**	**13**
	Information audit	14
	Information needs	18
	Research methods	23
	Task analysis	27
	Resource analysis	33
	User modelling	38
	Summary: a case study	41
	Further reading	45
	References	45
3	**Searching and finding**	**49**
	Search strategies	49
	Search features and search statements	53
	Finding	67

	Taxonomies	74
	Overview	89
	Further reading	90
	References	91
4	**Documents and document description**	**93**
	Document description and content analysis	94
	Metadata	100
	Dublin Core	104
	Thesaurus construction and ontologies	107
	Summary	117
	Further reading	117
	References	118
5	**Interface and display design**	**121**
	The human-computer interface	122
	Mental models and metaphors	124
	Interaction styles	127
	Basic design principles	133
	Display design	136
	Screen layout	138
	Navigation	144
	Graphics	154
	Colour	157
	Summary	162
	Further reading	163
	References	164
6	**Management and maintenance**	**167**
	Content management	167
	Content management strategy	171
	Management and maintenance issues	174

	Further reading	177
	References	177
7	**Evaluation**	**179**
	Objective measures of system effectiveness	182
	Evaluating information architectures	187
	Final thoughts on information architecture development	190
	Final thoughts on information architects	191
	References	193
Appendices		
	1 Dewey Decimal Schedules: extract	195
	2 Alphabetical listing	197
	3 Thesuarus entries	199
	4 Term tree	207
Index		**209**

List of abbreviations

ARMA   Association of Records Managers and Administrators

ASK   anomalous states of knowledge

ASSIA   Applied Social Services Index and Abstracts

BC   Bliss Bibliographic Classification

CMS   content management system

DDC   Dewey Decimal Classification

ERIC   Education Resources Information Center (US Department of Education)

GOMS   goals, operators, methods, selection

HCI   human-computer interaction/interface

HII   human-information interaction

INISS   Information Needs and Information Services in Local Authority Social Services Departments

LCC   Library of Congress Classification

MMI   man-machine interaction

OCLC   Online Computer Library Center

RNIB   Royal National Institute for the Blind

UDC   Universal Decimal Classification

W3C   World Wide Web Consortium

WIMP   window, icon, mouse, pointer/pull-down menu

List of figures

1.1   Animal kingdom classification   7

2.1   Information map – search for 'mapping information'   15

2.2   Information flows   22

2.3   Quantitative research questions   24

2.4   Qualitative research questions   25

2.5   Task analysis: cleaning teeth   29

2.6   Task analysis: buying a book   37–8

2.7   Personas   40

3.1   Features of searching and browsing   53

3.2   Disposal of hazardous substances   55

3.3   Search for 'hazardous substances disposal'   59

3.4   Search for 'disposal of hazardous substances'   60

3.5   Dialog search   61

3.6   Google Advanced Search   64

3.7   Dialog Bluesheets: some of the searchable fields in the
      Inspec database   65

3.8   Search features   66

3.9   Open Directory: home page   75

3.10 Open Directory: Reference category   77

3.11 Open Directory: Knowledge Management category   78

3.12 Open Directory: Information Architecture category   79

3.13 Polyhierarchies – Open Directory: Information Architecture
      catetgory   84

3.14 Open Directory: Web Usability   85

4.1 Content components: one document, many uses   99

4.2 Relationships   100

4.3 MARC21: outline   102

4.4 Dublin Core   105

4.5 Thesaurus entries: abbreviations and relationships   110

5.1 Microsoft Word toolbar   126

5.2 Internet Explorer toolbar   126

5.3 Dialog Classic command interface   128

5.4 DialogWeb command interface   129

5.5 Open Directory   131

5.6 Expedia.co.uk: home page   132

5.7 British Library: home page   140

5.8 British Library: intermediate navigation page (from the
     site map)   141

5.9 British Library: content page   142

5.10 bbc.co.uk: home page   143

5.11 Guardian.co.uk: home page   145

5.12 Guardian.co.uk: content page   146

5.13 TFPL: home page   147

5.14 Epicurious.com: home page   148

5.15 Open Directory: navigation links   150

5.16 BBC: A–Z   152

5.17 Firefox browser   153

5.18 Google: home page   155

5.19 Yahoo!: home page   156

5.20 London Metropolitan University: extranet home page   158

5.21 London Metropolitan University: intranet home page   159

6.1 McKeever's hierarchy   168

6.2 Information life cycle   170

7.1 Information architect: job titles   192

7.2 Information architecture: skills   193

Preface

This book examines the field of information architecture from the perspective of an information professional and is intended to explain concepts in a way that will be accessible to information professionals as well as to a wider readership. The aim is to explain information architecture partly within the context of traditional librarianship, and partly within the context of systems design. Subjects of relevance to the study of information architecture are varied and wide-ranging; this book does not claim to cover all aspects in depth, but to provide an overview of issues to the extent that basic theoretical and practical understanding is developed.

The text is arranged into six chapters:

- *Chapter 1: Information architecture: an introduction.* This chapter examines the scope of the subject and discusses the various ways in which information architecture has been defined. It goes on to examine core concepts of information architecture: indexing, classification, cataloguing and user-centred design.

- *Chapter 2: The preliminaries.* This chapter focuses upon the pre-design stages of developing information architectures. The ultimate use and effectiveness of an information system is dependent upon a thorough investigation of user needs, organisational needs, tasks and individual resources. Each of these areas is explained in detail, and the usefulness of various research methods is discussed. The summary demonstrates how the preliminary design stages feed into the overall systems development.

- *Chapter 3: Searching and finding.* This chapter focuses upon search and retrieval facilities. Specific search features are put into the context of the search strategy with an examination of analytical and browsing strategies. Then search engine features and taxonomy creation are examined in depth.

- *Chapter 4: Documents and document description.* Here the focus is on the information contained within the architecture. An explanation of records management and content analysis is followed by an examination of metadata creation and the Dublin Core Metadata Set. The chapter then concentrates on thesaurus construction as a means to control vocabulary and to map semantic relationships among subjects. This leads into a discussion of ontologies as a means of adding value to search and retrieval facilities.

- *Chapter 5: Interface and display design.* In this chapter we move away from information management to explore principles of interface design and usability. Basic concepts of human-computer interaction are outlined and discussed before concentrating upon designing screen layout, navigation features, graphics and use of colour and how they contribute to both efficiency and aesthetic appeal.

- *Chapter 6: Management and maintenance.* In this chapter the importance of strategy and policy in managing the development of the information architecture is discussed. Then the focus shifts to post-deployment issues. No matter how well designed the information architecture, its continuing value to an organisation relies upon it being well managed and well maintained. Roles and responsibilities are outlined within the context of management and maintenance issues.

- *Chapter 7: Evaluation.* In this chapter an overview of all the issues covered in the book is provided by examining evaluation research in general and evaluation criteria in particular. Finally, the range of jobs and job titles associated with information architecture is explored.

Screenshots are used throughout the text to illustrate features of systems, as well as supplementary text to further explain or illustrate points raised. For anyone wishing to explore concepts in greater depth, lists of supplementary readings are provided.

About the author

Sue Batley is a senior lecturer at London Metropolitan University and course director of the MA in Information Services Management. Having completed a PhD on factors affecting behaviour and retrieval of information from picture databases at the University of Aberdeen in 1989, Sue first worked as a subject librarian and lecturer at the University of East London, before taking up her current post in 1996. Her teaching and research centre upon the organisation and retrieval of information, covering traditional cataloguing and classification as well as information and knowledge architecture.

Sue is also the author of *Classification in Theory and Practice* published by Chandos in the Information Professional series in 2005.

The author may be contacted as follows:

E-mail: *s.batley@londonmet.ac.uk*

Information architecture: an introduction

Information architecture defined

If information architecture can be described as a discipline, it is not one with clearly defined boundaries. Reading the literature that uses the term in its title or in its text, it is possible to identify a whole range of topics, some clearly interrelated, some seemingly disparate, that contribute to the subject area. Adding to the confusion, it is clear that a lot of literature that does not explicitly claim to be about information architecture actually is. Given this rather chaotic picture, and the apparent fuzziness of the boundaries of the subject, it seems sensible to begin with an attempt to define the scope of the discipline or at least the scope of this book.

Information professionals should certainly be familiar with one of the central concepts, explained in Orna's definition: 'Information is what human beings transform their knowledge into when they want to communicate it to other people. It is knowledge made visible or audible, in written or printed words or in speech.'[1] Information is the content of books, journals, videos, presentations, e-mails, websites; it is the content of libraries, intranets and the World Wide Web. Information professionals deal with information in its various forms and from its various sources every day of their working lives. It is something very familiar, but that does not mean it is straightforward. Orna's definition, clearly from the viewpoint of an information professional, suggests the breadth of the concept. The 'information' in 'information architecture' might be the content of libraries, it might be published in books or journals, but it is more likely to be buried in a website or in an e-mail attachment or in a pile of papers sitting on someone's desk. The information we are really concerned with here is the information that is created by someone but not necessarily communicated to anyone else.

The other central concept, architecture, is about the built environment, the design of buildings and other structures. Architects design a framework and fill it with a series of interconnected functional spaces (rooms). Architecture in the sense we are interested in, in the context of information, has a long history, with Wurman[2] apparently first using the term 'information architect' in the 1970s. A long history does not, however, mean that there is agreement on what the architecture metaphor represents. Morville[3] points out that the term was originally being used in a rather restrictive sense: one that appealed more to the computer science community than the information community. Taking inspiration from the built environment again, Worple points out that: 'Architecture is concerned with more than just the frame, skin and external detailing of a building.'[4] This reminds us that architecture is not only about creating robust, attractive structures, it is also about what is contained within them: their functionality. In the context of this book, the architecture provides the structure, the information will determine functionality.

Terminology from architecture in the sense of the built environment is, not surprisingly, often used in definitions of information architecture. The Information Architecture Institute[5] defines information architecture as:

- the structural design of shared information environments;
- the art and science of organising and labelling websites, intranets, online communities and software to support usability and findability;
- an emerging community of practice focused on bringing principles of design and architecture to the digital landscape.

There are clear similarities here to the definitions offered by Rosenfeld and Morville:[6]

- the combination of organisation, labelling and navigation schemes within an information system;
- the architectural design of an information space to facilitate task completion and intuitive access to content;
- the art and science of structuring and classifying websites and intranets to help people find and manage information;
- an emerging discipline and community of practice focused on bringing principles of design and architecture to the digital landscape.

It cannot be assumed, though, that everyone is now in agreement about the scope of the subject area. Some authors would argue that information architecture is synonymous with taxonomy (see Rosenfeld and Morville's third definition above and the Wikipedia entry,[7] for example); this does not seem helpful as the taxonomy is only one part of the information environment. Content management systems (CMS) are often treated as being synonymous with information architecture in the literature; again this is a rather narrow perspective. There is also an increasing body of literature around knowledge architecture which appears to be exactly the same as information architecture but with an emphasis on knowledge sharing to increase the appeal to the corporate community.

So there is no single, straightforward definition of information architecture. Part of the reason for this probably lies in the fact that the discipline is, as pointed out in Rosenfeld and Morville's final definition, still emerging. But, when we start to pick apart the definitions offered, we can see common elements, particularly the concepts of organisation and design. We can now put this into the context of information architecture for information professionals: one aspect of the subject area is information management and its core elements – indexing, cataloguing and classification – recording and organising information. The second major area requiring treatment is design – specifically user-centred design – of information systems that support the needs of users by providing attractive, intuitive interfaces supporting a range of information tasks and accommodating a range of individual resources.

So far the focus has been upon what information architecture is; now we need to consider what it does. It is essentially concerned with increasing findability, which Morville defines as:

- the quality of being locatable or navigable;
- the degree to which a particular object is easy to discover or locate;
- the degree to which a system or environment supports navigation and retrieval.[8]

He points out that most business websites have major problems: poor information architecture, weak compliance with web standards, no metadata, content buried in databases that are invisible to search engines – in other words, poor findability.

Increasing findability is what information professionals do, that is the focus of our training. Information professionals act as intermediaries between the information held within an organisation or library and those who need to access that information. We facilitate access by organising and recording information and then providing tools and assistance to enhance its findability. Core concepts concerned with increasing findability are outlined in the next section.

Core concepts

As information professionals we already 'do' information architecture. Three of the four core concepts examined in this section, and throughout the book as a whole, should be very familiar to us: indexing, classification and cataloguing. The final core concept, user-centred design, may seem less familiar; we do not necessarily design and build information systems, but we certainly use them, and so have an understanding of key issues.

Indexes and indexing

An index is simply a guide that helps someone to locate information: locate either in the sense of finding it – on the page of a book, on a library shelf, on a website – or locate in the sense of providing confirmation that it exists. An index is usually made up of a series of headings or access points arranged in some recognisable order: alphabetical or numerical, for example. There are many different types of indexes and many books written about them; here we can concentrate on subject indexes and coordinate indexes, as they are of most relevance in the context of information architecture.

Alphabetical subject indexes consist of lists of subjects arranged alphabetically. That sounds very simple, but it is not necessarily as straightforward as it would appear. The first complication is in deciding how to name the subjects. Many different words might be used to represent the same concept – and an indexer has to take account of the different ways the various users of the index might describe the same basic subject. If a subject has more than one name, an index has to bring all material on that subject together, regardless of how it is named. That means there has to be allowance for synonyms, for example. A subject index will very often use a controlled vocabulary – a list of preferred terms which standardises the subject names used in the index and which defines ambiguous terms. Standardisation is important; one of the key issues in indexing is consistency – not just in using the same name consistently to describe the same subject, but also in, for example, use of word form and how compound headings are expressed throughout the index. Another important concept is referencing: 'use' or 'see' references to indicate equivalence relationships (synonyms) and 'related term' or 'see also' references to indicate associative relationships. Alphabetical subject indexes are not as straightforward as they might at first seem – although, like any other index, they ought to be straightforward to use. Issues around naming subjects, consistency and referencing are explored in the thesaurus construction and ontology sections of Chapter 4 on documents and document description.

Classified subject indexes display information in a taxonomy: expressing explicit relationships between subjects in a series of hierarchies; they attempt to map a subject area and to pull together related subjects based on an assumption of how knowledge is structured. Classified subject indexes have to be supplemented by an alphabetical subject index like a thesaurus because it cannot be assumed that the users of the classified index all share the same understanding of the structure of knowledge. The schedules of a traditional classification scheme are essentially a classified index. So, following on from that point, classified indexes should allow for browsing in exactly the same way that the physical library environment does. Classification is treated in more detail below.

Coordinate indexes are created by combining two or more index terms. They allow for compound subjects to be described and retrieved. Coordination of index terms can be done by a user as they are searching for information or by an indexer as items are being added to an information system for subsequent retrieval. Where coordination of terms is done by a user the indexes are post-coordinate, where it is done by an indexer they are pre-coordinate. In searching a post-coordinate index the user would construct a search statement using single keywords, simple phrases or Boolean operators – we have all used post-coordinate indexes when we have used a search engine like Google. In searching a pre-coordinate index the user would select a compound heading from a list compiled by an indexer – we have all used pre-coordinate indexes to find something in a book, and also if we have used web directories like those provided by Yahoo and the Open Directory (with their subject tree approach). Both types of index are examined in depth in Chapter 3 on searching and finding.

Classification

We have an innate ability to classify things. Classification is something we do all the time and we see examples of it all around us. We class one type of animal as a dog, another as a cat – we do not even have to think about it, it seems to be perfectly natural to differentiate between things in that way. We also classify things according to their relationship to each other, for example dogs and cats are more like each other than they are like budgerigars or goldfish. So at this level classification is unconscious, we classify things to simplify our world and make sense of it. Classification is simply about grouping together things which are alike; it is about imposing some sort of structure on our understanding of our environment. We all have our own personal classification of the world which we have developed through our experiences. One person might classify dogs under dangerous animals to be avoided; another person might classify dogs as friendly animals to have around the house.

The representation of how the biological sciences make sense of the animal kingdom is an example of a formal classification scheme (see Figure 1.1). The phyla are like the main classes in a library classification scheme. We can recognise similarities and differences between animals within a phylum, so we can subdivide to recognise these similarities and differences. Within the phylum chordata, there is a subphylum, vertebrata; within that subphylum there is a class, mammalia; within that class there is a subclass, theria; within that subclass there is an infraclass, eutheria. This is where the hierarchy stops, but we can continue to subdivide until we reach a point where we no longer have a group, we have an individual instance. Within the infraclass, eutheria, we recognise an order, primates; within that order there is a family, hominidae; within that family there is a genus, homo; within that genus there is a species, homo sapiens; within that species there is you. The whole point of classification is that we do not have to understand everything we experience as unique; we can place it within a structure that recognises its properties without having to make individual sense of it.

The animal kingdom classification is a complex example of a formal classification scheme. There are simple examples of formal classification schemes all around us: if you go into an off licence you will see that beers, wines and spirits are shelved separately and wines might be further classified into red and white, French, Italian, Australian and so on. All shops use classification to differentiate between the different types of goods they sell, because by doing so they are helping their customers to find what they want: they are organising their stock in a way which is helpful to their users.

So classification helps to organise, to make sense of things; it also helps to locate things. Library classification operates on that principle: it operates to keep similar items together and separate from dissimilar

Figure 1.1 Animal kingdom classification

Phylum	Subphylum	Class	Subclass	Infraclass
Protozoa				
Porifera				
Coelenterata				
Platyhelminthes				
Nematoda				
Mollusca		Cephalopoda		
		Lamellibranchia		
		Gastropoda		
Annelida				
Arthropoda		Insecta		
		Myriapoda		
		Arachnida		
		Crustacea		
Brachiopoda				
Chaetognatha				
Echinodermata				
Hemichordata				
Chordata	Urochordata			
	Cephalochordata			
	Vertebrata	Agnatha		
		Chondrichthyes		
		Amphibia		
		Reptilia		
		Aves		
		Mammalia	Prototheria	
			Theria	Metatheria
				Eutheria

items. It attempts to do this in a way which will help the library users to locate the materials they need: the aim is to get the book to the reader or the reader to the book in the quickest possible time. Library classification organises in two ways. First it organises knowledge by identifying similarities between subjects. Just like the animal kingdom classification, library classification schemes list the main and subsidiary branches of knowledge – so they provide a taxonomy of knowledge by dividing it into Social Sciences, Natural Sciences, Applied Sciences and so on. Second, library classification organises books on shelves. Library classification is supposed to show the distance between separate subjects by the distance between books on those subjects on the library shelves. So the library embodies a knowledge structure – it is a taxonomy represented in physical space. In this book we are more interested in virtual space but the principle is exactly the same. Classification is examined in depth in the sections on library classification and taxonomies.

Cataloguing

Charles Cutter defined the functions of a library catalogue in 1904. He wrote that it should:

1. Enable a person to find a book of which either:

   the author

   the title

   the subject

   is known.

2. Show what the library has:

   by a given author

   on a given subject

   in a given kind of literature.

3. Assist in the choice of a book:

   as to its edition

   as to its character (literary or topical).[9]

These rules still apply, except that the term record can be substituted for book and the term system for library. Cataloguing focuses on the content of an information store. It provides a framework for describing all the items present in a collection and facilitates their effective management and retrieval. Libraries could not function without catalogues; information systems cannot function without effective records management, at the heart of which is document analysis and description. These issues are examined in depth in Chapter 4 on documents and document description.

The cataloguing process basically consists of two operations in the context of information architecture: the creation of a description relating to a particular electronic document, and the manipulation of all the individual descriptions of all the e-documents to form an index or database. The focus in this book is on the creation of the document descriptions which comprise the index entries: humans provide the descriptions, software performs the manipulation. Traditional library cataloguing, using standards as set out in the Anglo-American Cataloguing Rules and MARC21 formats, generates bibliographic descriptions that identify specific bibliographic resources. These same standards, which essentially generate metadata, can be used to generate descriptions for digital resources, but they are far too detailed and formalised to be widely applied. In information architecture cataloguing becomes metadata creation and the closest equivalent to the MARC formats is the Dublin Core Metadata Element set. Cataloguing of digital resources is examined in detail in the section on metadata.

User-centred design

Having gathered our collection of digital information resources, having named our subjects and created an index or thesaurus to provide vocabulary control, having applied classification theory to impose a logical structure on our resources, and having created metadata to describe individual e-documents, we are now concerned with ensuring that the interface to our information system meets the needs of our various users. So we use the outcomes of our needs analysis, task analysis and resource analysis and apply principles of user-centred systems design when constructing our system.

Interestingly, given the number of books available on website design and the large body of literature on HCI – Human-Computer Interaction or Human-Computer Interface – there are lots of very poorly designed websites and information systems. We do not only find examples of poor design in the digital environment of course. Donald Norman, for example, often makes the point that good design is not so difficult to achieve, so why are we surrounded by examples of poor design? In *The Design of Everyday Things*,[10] Norman looks at microwave ovens, washing machines and swing doors, but the points he raises about their design are universal principles that translate easily into the digital environment.

There is really no point at all in creating an elegant information structure and a comprehensive index of resources if it is poorly represented at the interface to the system. So in this book we look at ways to increase usability of digital information systems – to make them user-centred. As noted previously architecture is not only about creating robust structures, it is also about functionality and it is also about aesthetic appeal. These issues are explored in depth in Chapter 5 on interface and display design.

Summary

This chapter has outlined the scope of information architecture and its core concepts. It should be clear from this introduction to the subject that information professionals, whatever information environment they operate within, already, to at least some extent, practise information architecture. This book, written from the perspective of an information professional, aims to provide a practical approach to developing, evaluating and managing information systems in a way that will be understood by and appeal to the library and information management community. In a single book that aims to look at all relevant aspects of information architecture, the treatment of some subjects is necessarily brief, but in all cases essential principles are outlined and suggestions for further reading will allow for more in-depth exploration of the areas covered.

Further reading

There are many books covering the core concepts outlined in this chapter, for anyone wishing to explore indexing, classification and cataloguing from a library perspective in more depth, the following are recommended:

- Batley, S. (2005) *Classification in Theory and Practice*. Oxford: Chandos.
- Bowman, J.H. (2002) *Essential Cataloguing*. London: Facet.
- Lancaster, F.W. (2003) *Indexing and Abstracting in Theory and Practice*, rev. edn. London: Facet.

Coverage of all three areas is provided in:

- Chowdhury, G.G. (2004) *Introduction to Modern Information Retrieval*, 2nd edn. London: Facet.
- Rowley, J. and Farrow, J. (2000) *Organizing Knowledge*, 3rd edn. Aldershot: Gower.

Taking a broader approach to information technologies than offered in this book and providing an in-depth analysis of the concept of findability, the following is highly recommended:

- Morville, P. (2006) *Ambient Findability*. Sebastopol, CA: O'Reilly.

References

1. Orna, E. (2004) *Information Strategy in Practice*. Aldershot: Gower, p. 7.
2. Wurman, R.S. (1996) *Information Architects*. New York: Graphis.
3. Morville, P. (2004) 'A brief history of information architecture', in A. Gilchrist and B. Mahon (eds), *Information Architecture: Designing Information Environments for Purpose*. London: Facet.
4. Worple, K. (2000) *The Value of Architecture: Design, Economy and the Architectural Imagination*. London: RIBA Future Studies.
5. Information Architecture Institute: *http://iainstitute.org/pg/about_us.php* (accessed 28 August 2006).
6. Rosenfeld, L. and Morville, P. (2002) *Information Architecture for the World Wide Web*. Sebastopol, CA: O'Reilly, p. 4.
7. Wikipedia: *http://en.wikipedia.org/wiki/Information_architecture* (accessed 28 August 2006).
8. Morville, P. (2006) *Ambient Findability*. Sebastopol, CA: O'Reilly, p. 4.
9. Cutter, C.A. (1904) *Rules for a Dictionary Catalog*, 4th edn. Washington, DC: Government Printing Office.
10. Norman, D.A. (2002) *The Design of Everyday Things*. New York: Basic Books.

The preliminaries

In the previous chapter we have seen that the field of information architecture encompasses a wide range of topics, from basic concepts of information management to interface design. The aim of information architecture is to create well-structured, attractive and, once deployed, well-maintained information systems that allow users to search for and retrieve information quickly and efficiently. An essential point to note is that the information architecture exists to serve the needs of its users. This means that system development has to be underpinned by a deep understanding of those users – the people who will access the system to search for and retrieve the information that they need. A deep understanding of the users can only be developed by conducting a thorough needs, task and resource analysis, after which it should be possible to start to design an information system that is truly user-centred. These preliminary stages that will underpin the eventual system architecture are what we concentrate on in this chapter.

In designing information systems, it is possible to identify four preliminary stages that feed into the design process:

- *Information needs analysis* – find out what information the users of the system need access to. This involves discovering what problems they face and what information they need to resolve those problems. Needs analysis feeds into system design: information and features that people have to access on a regular basis should be represented at or near the surface of the system architecture; it also feeds into content management.

- *Task analysis* – find out what the users of the system do when they are attempting to satisfy their information needs. This takes us into the field of search behaviour and the development of search strategies. Most searching and finding strategies involve a combination of analytical and browsing tasks. It is important that users have a range of search and browsing features available to them to maximise the efficiency of their interactions with the system. It is also important that simple tasks are simple to execute.

- *Resource analysis* – find out what knowledge and practical skills, for example, the users of the system employ as they complete their tasks. A user-centred system should cater for a whole range of personal competencies and accommodate individual preferences.

- *User modelling* – identify different categories of users based on their needs, the tasks they perform and the resources they use to complete the tasks. This simplifies the process of designing the system to accommodate individual needs.

This chapter is structured around these four themes.

Information audit

Needs, task and resource analysis falls under the umbrella of the information audit, needs assessment or knowledge inventory. Dubois explains that the information audit within the context of a commercial organisation 'allows the resources devoted to information to be mapped, analysed, costed and rationalised … At the same time undocumented formal and informal communication flows may be revealed which can contribute to the development of optimal management structures.'[1]

A search on the web will reveal a lot of companies offering consultancy and expertise in this area. The description of the information audit cited below is taken from the website of one of these, TFPL. An information audit can be described as:

> A systematic process through which an organisation can understand its knowledge and information needs, what it knows, the information flows and gaps. Resulting from an information audit is an 'information map' which can be used as the basis for designing the content of intranets, as well as for the foundation of a corporate information strategy or a knowledge management strategy.[2]

Most definitions of information audit refer to an information map or information mapping. It is useful to explain this further.

Alternative names for information maps include concept maps and mind maps. The Kartoo metasearch engine displays results as an information map (see Figure 2.1). All results for a search are clustered on

Figure 2.1 Information map – search for 'mapping information'

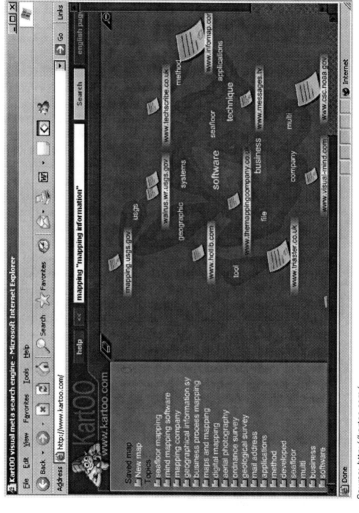

Source: http://kartoo.com/

the basis of similarity. These clusters, listed on the left side of the Kartoo results screen, are then displayed as an information or concept map. In the example in Figure 2.1 'software' is the dominant concept – in fact most of the results for the query 'mapping information' are about information mapping software. In an organisation's information map the clusters would represent departments, functions, operational areas and so on. Some clusters would be central to the organisation's interests and would appear at the centre of the map, others would be sited on the basis of their importance to the organisation.

The information map is mentioned quite casually in TFPL's description of the information audit, but Evernden and Evernden note that 'a detailed enterprise information map or model will take between 2 and 5 years to develop.'[3] Fortunately they also point out that generic models are widely available and that 80 per cent of the information map will be the same across organisations; it is the 20 per cent that is unique to a particular organisation that can be the focus of research.

It is, in any event, clear that the information audit has to focus on the needs of a particular organisation and every organisation will be different. Even in the case of organisations offering similar services or products it will be possible to identify differences in the way information is utilised and how it flows, for example. An information audit will examine a specific case and seek to provide specific solutions. It is something that most companies will engage in as they seek to manage and exploit their information and knowledge resources. Even though the definitions cited above have a corporate focus, it has to be emphasised that this is not something that is only of value in the commercial sector – organisations in all sectors are keen to maximise use of digital information resources to improve communication and to improve services.

So, the information audit will attempt to identify what information is created and needed across an organisation. Specifically, the information audit will identify the following:

- *The information needs of the whole organisation, the information needs of various departments within the organisation and the specific needs of individuals within the organisation.* It is not possible to address organisational needs without considering the needs of individuals within that organisation – the information audit has to examine all levels of needs.

- *The information created within the organisation and its value.* The information audit is often conducted within the context of knowledge management, where knowledge, information and skills are perceived as having a real monetary value to the organisation. However, this applies just as much to service industries where the services themselves have value to customers. This leads to the next point.

■ *Expertise and knowledge assets* – owned by individual people within the organisation. The information audit should identify ways in which individuals can best utilise their skills to achieve their full potential and to maximise their value to the organisation.

■ *Information gaps* – what is missing? Do people need information that is not readily available to them? This is clearly very important. If poor access to information and knowledge resources is affecting people's performance then steps need to be taken to correct the problem. Mapping information flow (see below) might help here by identifying blockages and information bottlenecks.

■ *External information resources and how they may be used more effectively.* In terms of information media this will include a range of 'traditional' resources – the contents of libraries or information services – and also digital resources – databases, websites, e-journals and e-book collections for example. Other organisations and individuals providing services or skills can also be included here.

■ *Internal information resources, how valuable they are and how they might be better utilised.* Again, an information service, internally generated documents and individual knowledge and skills can be included here.

■ *Information flows* – how information is disseminated throughout the organisation. This is discussed in more detail below.

It is clear then that the scope of the information audit is very wide-ranging and to conduct it properly requires a lot of time, effort and, of course, money. To make such a large-scale investment an organisation must be convinced of the benefits. It is suggested that an organisation will engage in an information audit because they think it can help them to:

■ make better use of intellectual assets;
■ make better use of external information;
■ avoid inefficiencies and duplication of information;
■ avoid information overload;
■ save time and money through efficiencies.[4]

This last point is an important one. Most organisations engage in the information audit because they think it can help them to become more profitable. This goes back to the commercial focus mentioned earlier, but of course all organisations, whatever sector they are in, want to be more efficient and cost-effective. Designing better information systems is not specifically mentioned here, but elements of the information audit will certainly help in that respect. It can certainly be argued that information audit has to feed into systems design – and a good, user-centred information system, focusing on individual and organisational needs, can improve information and knowledge sharing and lead to better service provision.

Information needs

Cognitive aspects

Before we examine organisational needs analysis, it is important to consider cognitive aspects of information need as this helps in understanding the complexity of the concept. It has already been noted that the information need of the user is of central concern to providers of information systems and services. The ultimate aim of any information system is to supply and deliver the information which its users require. The importance of this cannot be underestimated because the success of the whole information and knowledge transfer process depends largely on the accurate identification of what the user needs.

So, it is the function of information systems to attempt to satisfy the information needs of their users. This, at a superficial level, would appear to be relatively straightforward. Users follow hyperlinks to find answers to questions or users formulate queries and the system responds. But it is not as simple as this would make it appear: the concept of information need is, as previously noted, an extremely complex one. A need for information is not a concrete thing and it very often cannot be easily identified and objectified or expressed. It is not always easy to define or express what information is needed. In other words, the answer the user is seeking or the query the user formulates might not be an accurate representation of what they actually need.

A problem with any consideration of information need is that the term itself is very imprecise. Maurice Line attempted to rid the term of its ambiguity by differentiating between the following:

- Need
- Want

- Demand
- Use.[5]

Line suggests that it is helpful to think of need in terms of 'what an individual ought to have, for his work, his research, his edification, his recreation, etc.' A 'want', on the other hand, is 'what an individual would like to have'. Demand is what is often assumed to be the literal expression of the need. Demand is 'what an individual asks for ... Individuals may demand information they do not need, and certainly need or want information they do not demand.' Use is, of course, 'what an individual actually uses'. Line goes on to suggest that 'requirement' is a more accurate term, and more expressive of the concept, than 'need'.

This is not simply an empty debate about semantics, it is central to systems design. A lot of studies that purport to be about information 'needs' have actually been concerned with information 'demands' and information 'uses'. We assume that what users ask for or what they use is what they actually need, when in fact they tend to ask for what they expect the system to provide and use what is at hand. So what we assume is an information need has been compromised by user expectations of the information system and current provision. This is a dangerous assumption because people may 'need' something that they do not ask for or that the information system cannot provide. The problem for information architects is in making sure that the systems they design are structured around, and will support, information needs.

Why defining needs should be such a problem lies within the sphere of cognitive psychology and requires further explanation. A lot of studies of information needs and their expression focused on the interactions between the library user and the librarian or information professional and concentrated on the interviewing skills needed by the librarian to elicit the true need for information. With the development of expert intermediary and then end-user online searching, studies began to focus on systems rather than libraries. A lot of important literature in this area was produced in the 1960s and 1970s; it is still relevant.

A need for information arises when someone is aware that they lack the knowledge or understanding to achieve some goal: to answer a question, write a report and so on. This awareness of a gap in understanding can initiate interaction with an information system. An important distinction to make is between an original, perceived need for information and the user's articulation of that need – how they express the need in searching within, or querying, the information system.

Taylor defined four stages in the development of an information need:

1. The actual, but unexpressed, need – which Taylor called the visceral need.

2. The conscious need – when the user becomes aware of the need for information.

3. The formalised need – when the user defines the need.

4. The compromised need – the query as presented to the information system.[6]

This four-stage process emphasises the distance between the original, actual need and the final articulated one. A fundamental problem in the information transfer process is the user's ability, or inability, to communicate their need for information. If the communication process between user and system breaks down at any point then the system will be unable to provide the information the user needs. In order for interaction with an information system to be successful, an individual must first be aware of a gap in their knowledge, must then be aware of the information system's ability to assist them in filling the gap in understanding, and must then be able to communicate what information is needed. Belkin[7] wrote about anomalous states of knowledge (ASK). He pointed out that an information need arises from a recognised anomaly in someone's state of knowledge concerning some topic or situation – an awareness of a gap in understanding. Their lack of understanding means that, in general, the user is unable to specify precisely what they need to resolve the anomaly. Simply stated, ASK is about knowing you need something but not knowing how to ask for it. If you do not know something, you will find it very difficult to describe exactly what it is you do not know – you will not have the understanding or the vocabulary to do it.

It is also important to realise that just as the user's state of knowledge is dynamic – it changes – so the need for information is dynamic – as the user starts to find information and understand the problem better, their ability to articulate their needs can be expected to change. In the initial stages of a search for information, users are most likely to express the need for information in the form of questions which relate to their existing knowledge. It is only when specific gaps in knowledge have been identified that users can be expected to express their needs in more specific terms. Obviously, the more you understand about a problem, the better able you are to solve it.

We will return to the problems associated with discovering and defining information needs in the section on research methods.

Organisational aspects

Now the focus moves back to the information audit and to the process of information needs analysis within an organisation. Information systems and services have to be designed to meet the needs of users within organisations. It is not possible to design effective user-centred information systems and services without a thorough analysis of the needs of the people who will be using them. So, there is still a focus on the individual here, but information needs analysis at an organisational level has to take a broader view. Organisational needs analysis is not simply about what information individuals within an organisation need to work effectively, which is what we have concentrated on in considering the personal, cognitive aspects of need; rather it is about the environment within which the information system is located and, very importantly, within which its users are located. So information needs analysis is concerned with studying information in a broader, organisational context.

Information needs analysis tends to perceive the individual user as part of the whole organisational environment. It assumes that their individual information needs will develop through their interactions with that environment, and that by understanding the environment we can predict and characterise their needs. This makes very good sense. No one exists in a vacuum; we are all part of a wider social and organisational group. Our actions and interactions are to a large extent socially determined. For an information system to be effective and to truly meet the needs of its individual users, there has to be an awareness of its social and organisational context. Information needs analysis goes beyond thinking about what documents or factual information people within an organisation may need. It is about looking at the total range of information systems and services that may be appropriate in meeting the needs of users.

How do we go about analysing an organisation's information needs? First, as already suggested, we need to understand the total environment. A useful first step is to map information flow within the organisation, then to ask: what are the channels of communication? how does information transfer take place?

A simple model of information flow within a traditional hierarchically structured organisation will show information flowing in three directions (see Figure 2.2): from the top down, from the bottom up and horizontally within the levels of the organisation. Already here we are moving away from traditional information science, which tended to be concerned with a restricted horizontal flow of information: communication among and for specialist groups. A common problem in

Figure 2.2 Information flows

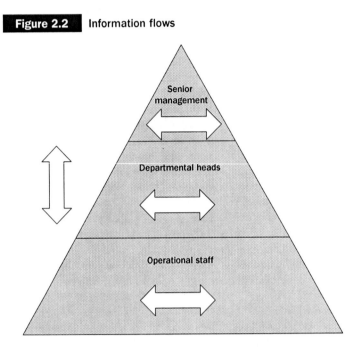

organisations of all sizes is that information does not flow smoothly between specialist groups or departments. Any information system has to ensure that information flows freely in all directions and, crucially, that it flows across departmental or specialist group boundaries.

The channels through which information is communicated have changed. A very obvious example is the increasing use of electronic media as opposed to paper. This does not simply refer to formal publications. E-mail is probably the most important communication medium in any organisation today. Also, it is easy to neglect the very important role of oral communication in information transfer. Something else that we have to bear in mind is that the organisation itself is part of a wider environment. Information flows into and out of the organisation as well as within it – communication channels have to connect the organisation to the outside world. In other words, the organisation is an open system rather than a closed one.

So in simply highlighting some very fundamental issues, several areas of concern in providing an information system which can meet user needs have been identified:

- Ensuring that information flows effectively within the organisation in at least three directions: up, down and horizontally, although a network or matrix structure better embodies the complexity of information flows. An information map can be adapted to display information flows and highlight blockages and bottlenecks.

- Ensuring that information is transmitted via the appropriate channels: via electronic media, paper media and orally.

- Acknowledging that the organisation is an open system, and that information transfer takes place, not only within the organisation, but also into and out of the organisation.

Having mapped information flow and examined channels of communication and information transfer, the next stage in the process of information needs analysis is to find answers to at least three questions:

- How does the present system operate?

- What do users require from a new system?

- What must be done to ensure the new system is being used effectively by everyone who should be using it?

Basically, what do we do now? What should we be doing? What are the implications for our users and our resources? Resources here encompass money, training for information service staff and training for users. How we might set about finding answers to these questions is examined in the next section.

Research methods

This is an area that has generated vast amounts of literature that it is not possible to cover in any depth here. Further readings around research methodologies and research design are provided at the end of this chapter for those wanting to explore this area further. Here the discussion is focused on basic techniques and their value in needs analysis.

There are two approaches to conducting research, quantitative and qualitative. Each methodology is associated with different research tools, each will generate different types of data that will be capable of different types of analysis: statistical or semantic. Quantitative methods aim for breadth and will generate data that can be analysed numerically, they are argued to be quicker and easier than qualitative methods. Using questionnaires, structured interviews and structured observation will usually generate quantitative data. The main disadvantage of conducting quantitative research is that it tends not to take account of the organisational environment. Rohde states: 'The quantitative approach with its emphasis on numbers and its quest for generalisation is seen as depersonalising information provision and information use and isolating them from the settings in which they occur.'[8] The problem is that this sort of survey, using questionnaires distributed to all personnel for example, while helpful for eliciting information about individual opinion, does not properly take environmental factors into account.

If a questionnaire with a series of closed questions is distributed to staff or used in interviewing them (see Figure 2.3), the resulting data is unlikely to be of much help in designing a new information system or improving an existing system. Ask people to rate existing services and systems and you may discover that they are not rated very highly, so you will have discovered a problem, but it is unlikely that you will be able to use that data in finding a solution to the problem. Monitor use of existing systems and services and you will generate data about demands and uses, but again you will not have discovered anything about 'needs'.

This suggests that questionnaires, structured interviews and structured observation are of only limited value. They provide quantitative data which can be used to justify change, but will actually tell you very little about the needs of the organisation. You may find that 75 per cent of respondents rarely use or never use the taxonomy, which is useful to know, but it is much more important to know why the taxonomy is not

Figure 2.3 Quantitative research questions

How often do you use the intranet?

    Daily   Weekly   Monthly   Never

How important to you is having access to Emerald Full-Text from your computer?

    Not important   Somewhat important   Extremely important

How do you rate the library collection?

    Poor   Satisfactory   Good   Excellent   Don't know being used. It could be that people did not know there was a taxonomy, or that it is poorly structured, or that it is poorly maintained, or that the information they need is not accessible via category selection. The type of questionnaire used in quantitative research tells you *what* but does not tell you *why*. Quantitative data do not really provide the type of information required to re-evaluate information systems in a broader organisational context. So what other methods are available?

There has been a move away from quantitative to qualitative research methods, or at least a move towards combining the two methodologies. Qualitative research aims for depth. Techniques meriting further consideration are open questionnaires (see Figure 2.4), naturalistic observation, depth interviews and focus groups. In terms of time and effort these techniques are much more costly and labour-intensive than structured questionnaires, interviews and observation. But if you really want to elicit information that can be used to re-evaluate or redesign your system these techniques are more likely to give you that information.

There is, of course still a potential problem here. Ask people what they need and, going back to Line's definitions, they are most likely to tell you what they want. A carefully designed study, using a mix of methods, will minimise this problem. Qualitative research will often include the use of an open-ended questionnaire. A study by Atwood and Dervin in 1981[9] used a three-part questionnaire. The first part dealt with problems, worries and concerns experienced by people over the previous month. The second part dealt with how a particular concern was handled or resolved. The third part asked how the participant would deal with four hypothetical situations. In asking about real work-based situations in which information was needed to resolve a problem, Attwood and Dervin's qualitative research technique aimed to elicit information about the users' information needs and how they set about satisfying them. In asking about specific work or task-related situations, you can find out a great deal about user needs and how they are satisfied.

Figure 2.4   Qualitative research questions

How would you find information about research funding?

Which journals do you need access to?

When did you last use the intranet, and why?

Project INISS (Information Needs and Information Services in Local Authority Social Services Departments)[10, 11] used a mix of qualitative and quantitative methods to investigate the information needs of staff in social services departments, the aim being to come up with ideas on how best to meet those needs. The research team began by visiting some social service departments with the aim to get a better understanding of their structures and their existing information services. So the first step was naturalistic observation (qualitative). The research team then used structured observation, followed by structured interviewing (quantitative).

It has to be pointed out that observation is a very time-consuming process. There is the observation itself, which ought to take place over at least several days or weeks; then there is the huge amount of data it generates, which then has to be analysed and categorised in some way. It is also, arguably, the best way to understand operational and management processes. In Project INISS the observation guided the structure of the interview phase. Wilson et al. state:

> One of our basic assumptions is that information needs must be placed in the context of the ordinary working life of the subjects under investigation. The observational phase of the work provided a detailed qualitative analysis of the nature of this work and the interviews concentrated upon three aspects only:
>
> - The specialist knowledge possessed by the interview subjects;
> - The extent to which this knowledge was exchanged with others; and
> - The effect of organisational climate on information transfer.[12]

This is very interesting, given the research was done over 25 years ago, because it highlights issues that have become very fashionable in the last ten years with the rise of knowledge management.

Wilson's methodology and the aims of his research are reflected in what is offered by consultancies today. TFPL, for example, who offer information audit services to organisations, state that:

> A successful information audit must reflect the organisation and how it works. It must review the different business processes within the organisation, exploring what information is needed in the process and what information is generated by the process. It requires a top-down as well as a bottom-up approach looking at all the information flows, barriers, and inefficiencies. To achieve all

the objectives of the information audit, to gather all the data, and to develop practical proposals, a mix of interviews, questionnaires, discussion groups and focus groups needs to be used.[13]

So TFPL recognises the importance of a mix of quantitative and qualitative methods.

The problem for a lot of organisations is that all this is very time-consuming and costly. There is a temptation to jump straight into designing the information system without examining organisational context and needs. There is software available that will assist in designing and implementing something that looks very professional and sophisticated. The temptation may be too much for some organisations. They can invest in software that will perform automatic taxonomy creation and search engine creation and then mount the result on their intranet and/or extranet. Six months later they may be dismayed to find out that no one is using the information system. If they had performed a needs analysis at the outset, they might have discovered that most information transfer takes place orally and that all that was needed to improve communication was a new telephone directory. That is obviously an extreme example, but there are certainly a lot of information systems out there that do not meet the needs of their users. It is vitally important to understand the context before designing the system.

Task analysis

As well as examining information needs the information audit should seek to discover what people do as they attempt to satisfy those needs. In systems design the aim is to match task demands with the knowledge and skills resources of the system users. So although tasks and individual resources can be considered separately, which is the approach adopted here, they are of course intimately related. Marshall makes this clear when he writes:

> For effective human-computer interaction, the procedures involved in achieving a given task should be compatible with the known cognitive characteristics of the user. Tasks and procedures should be structured logically and consistently but, more importantly, in a manner which is acceptable to the users and meets with their existing knowledge expectations.[14]

Good systems design requires careful task analysis. Norman cites an instance when he met with a software developer to discuss a widely used product and it became clear why there were so many problems with it:

> They kept adding new features, but they had never studied just what patterns of activities their customers performed, just what tasks needed to be supported. Tasks and activities are not well supported by isolated features. They require attention to the sequence of actions, to the eventual goal – that is, to the true needs.[15]

A problem for designers is that when even the simplest of tasks is broken down into its individual elements or sub-tasks, the picture quickly becomes very complex. Figure 2.5 is a rather frivolous example, but it does illustrate quite effectively how everything we do is composed of a series of discrete operations, most of which we do not even think about as we are completing the overall task. The point is that we do not have to think about the individual operations or sub-tasks assuming everything is at hand to support them. In this example, completion of the task is dependent upon having a toothbrush, having toothpaste and having water – as long as we have those facilities we can complete the task.

This kind of task analysis, perhaps surprisingly, actually translates very easily into the information systems environment. The system has to support all of the operations the execution of which will allow the user to complete their task or satisfy their need for information. However, information tasks are more complex than cleaning your teeth. It is easy to assume that everyone would use a toothbrush, toothpaste and water to clean their teeth. On the other hand, two users, even when searching for the same information, may use different search features and perform different operations in completing the task or conducting the search. If a user needs to find a document on a particular subject, then the system has to allow the user to type in a subject name or select a subject category in a taxonomy, for example. An information system, if it is to be truly user-centred, has to incorporate a range of different search facilities, support a range of information tasks and allow for individual differences.

To complicate matters further, it is possible to differentiate between generic and device-dependent tasks. Returning to the above example, the generic task may be maintaining oral hygiene; cleaning your teeth is device-dependent, requiring water, a toothbrush and toothpaste. In the context of information architecture, generic tasks would include concepts like searching, processing and communicating; device-dependent tasks would include use of search facilities like Boolean and phrase searching,

Figure 2.5   Task analysis: cleaning teeth

Pick up the tooth brush

Wet the brush

Take the cap off the tube

Put paste on the brush

Brush the outside of the bottom row of teeth

Brush the outside of the top row of teeth

Brush the biting surface of the top row of teeth

Brush the biting surface of the bottom row of teeth

Brush the inside surface of the bottom row of teeth

Brush the inside surface of the top row of teeth

Spit

Rinse the brush

Replace the brush in the holder

Grasp cup

Fill cup with water

Rinse teeth with water

Spit

Replace cup in holder

Wipe mouth on sleeve

Screw cap back on tube

Place tube in holder

Source: http://www.behavioradvisor.com/TaskAnalysis.html

category selection in a taxonomy and so on. Both types of task are of interest here, although the emphasis is on device-dependent tasks.

Allen says that:

> The goal of system design is to allow users to complete the tasks that will meet their information needs. With this in mind, system features that will augment the resources of users when necessary will enable them to complete the tasks. Some of these features will be required by all users, while others will be required by only a portion of the user group.[16]

Basically, the system has to allow users to interact with it in a variety of ways. It has to support a range of information tasks and it has to accommodate individual preferences. Individual preferences will be examined in more detail when we focus on resource analysis in the next section.

Task analysis involves breaking down the whole process of interacting with a system into a series of discrete tasks and it also involves examining the search tactics employed by users. In seeking for and finding information we develop search strategies. The search strategy is comprised of all the actions we take to complete an information search. Those individual actions are information search tactics. Some search tactics seem so informal and so natural that we do not even recognise them as part of the search strategy. Talking to people is a tactic, looking at general sources like a telephone directory or a glossary is a tactic. These less formal tactics, although easy to disregard, are arguably as important in the search process as typing a query at the system interface. The primary focus here is the search tactics supported by the information system, but in reality task analysis would also include less formal tactics like those noted above.

It is appropriate to introduce Kuhlthau's model of the information search process,[17] which we will return to in Chapter 3 on searching and finding, within the context of task analysis as it incorporates the behavioural aspects of the information search process. Her model includes three realms: the affective, the cognitive and the physical. It reminds us that good systems design relies upon a combination of aesthetics, clarity and efficiency. The task analysis should highlight how her three realms impact on information searching and finding.

The affective realm is concerned with how people feel; it is a term from psychology which is also associated with information need. This is actually very important in systems design – an unattractive screen display, for example, can have a big impact on system use. If the task analysis shows that some system features or facilities are under-utilised it could be that people simply do not like them. Use of these features might be encouraged by improving their aesthetic appeal.

The cognitive realm relates to the problem-solving that the searcher is engaging in – understanding the problem and understanding ways in which to interact with the system to solve the problem. Task analysis should reveal whether people are utilising information systems efficiently. If they are not, then training programmes and onscreen help facilities can assist users in better understanding how systems can support the completion of their information tasks.

The physical realm relates to actions – clicking on hyperlinks, typing in commands at a workstation, discussing information requirements with colleagues. Task analysis may reveal that simple operations, like sending an e-mail, require a disproportionately large amount of physical effort. In Chapter 3 on searching and finding we will see that this can impact on the use of a taxonomy – with users being reluctant to drill down to lower levels of the hierarchy – three or four mouse clicks and they will tend to abandon the search if they have not found what they need.

Marchionini suggests that completion of an information task can be divided into five broad areas that have an impact on systems design:

- Defining the problem
- Selecting the source
- Articulating the problem
- Examining the results
- Extracting the information.[18]

These five broad areas can be defined as generic tasks. We have already looked at defining the problem when we examined information needs and needs analysis. We can assume that the source is the organisation's information systems and services. Articulating the problem and examining the results are treated in depth in Chapter 3 on searching and finding. Extracting the information can be helped by good display design – which is examined in depth in Chapter 5 on interface and display design. Even though Marchionini's five points are examined in detail elsewhere in this book, they merit further consideration here. Each of Marchionini's five areas or generic tasks can be broken down further – he provides the framework, but we can go into a lot more detail by examining associated device-dependent tasks for articulating the problem and examining the results.

In the context of an information system, individual device-dependent tasks associated with articulating the problem would be supported by the provision of a range of search and browsing facilities that would allow for a range of tactics from the very basic to the highly sophisticated. For example:

- Can the user search on a single key term?
- Does the system support full Boolean searching?
- Does the system recognise phrases?
- Can the search be restricted to certain fields in a record?
- Can the user limit the search by date, format, etc.?

- Does the system automatically search for synonyms and plurals?

- Does the system support browsing activities through category selection?

Device-dependent tasks associated with examining the results would again be supported by system features. For example:

- Are results presented clearly so that they can be quickly scanned by the user?

- How are results ordered or grouped? By relevance, by date, alphabetically? Can the user change the presentation order?

- Can the user open documents directly from the results display?

- Can the user access the full text of a document to read directly from the results display?

- Can the user save a document on their workstation or network area?

- Can the user return easily to the results display after examining a document?

The team conducting the task analysis should already know which features are present, and can use their analysis to discover which of those features are used and how they are used. It may be that some features are under-utilised because they are not necessary – remember Norman's point about designing to support tasks and sequences of actions. Simply because certain features are supported by applications does not mean that they have to be present on the system.

So how would you conduct a task analysis? First of all, it is essential to find out what people would be using the system for – by conducting a needs analysis. From this, it will probably be possible to identify a series of representative tasks – things like: send an e-mail, access financial data, access personnel records, post information to a e-bulletin board, find a specific publication, find information about a particular subject, and so on. Next would be a process of observation and questioning to find out how people performed these tasks. This is sometimes termed high-level task decomposition, where these representative tasks are being broken down into their sub-tasks or operations and examining the tactics that people use in completing the tasks.

A good way to do this, if the purpose is to improve an existing system, is to sit with users and ask them to talk through what they are doing as they are interacting with the information system. This will also feed into the resource analysis in allowing you to identify individual differences in how people interact with the system, for example. Also, in asking people to talk through their information tasks, it is possible to not only identify what system features are used and how they are used, but also to identify what features people do not use and what features they would like that are not currently supported.

Resource analysis

When you have identified the tasks associated with attempting to satisfy a need for information and the tactics or sub-tasks people perform during the process of search and retrieval, you should go on to identify the resources they use when completing the tasks. This does not mean resources in terms of printed and electronic information sources, but personal resources. People will possess different resources in terms of their knowledge, skills and aptitudes. It is useful to consider resources in terms of individual knowledge, organisational knowledge and individual differences.

Individual knowledge is a valuable asset in any organisation. One of the main drivers for developing and improving information systems is to allow for more effective knowledge sharing. Individual knowledge also has a significant impact on how people use information systems. Many studies of search behaviour and of learning strategies and systems design stress the fact that people's behaviour is strongly determined by what they already know. So your existing knowledge determines how you approach a search for information, how you interact with systems and how you make sense of new information. It should be pretty obvious that your existing knowledge of a subject or your knowledge of an information system is going to affect the nature of your information need and the level of skill you apply in using the system to satisfy your information need.

In the literature you will often find a differentiation between semantic and procedural knowledge, which can be rather simplistically defined as theoretical versus practical knowledge. As information specialists we possess a lot of procedural knowledge. We know how to interact efficiently with information systems in order to extract information. So, for example, we can search Dialog for information on topics we are not familiar with. We know that we have to select and load a database or databases, we know that we interrogate the database using Dialog commands, we know how to construct a search statement using Boolean and phrase operators, limits and so on. We are expert in the procedure, but we may not have the semantic knowledge to judge whether the search results are relevant or not. Someone with the semantic knowledge to integrate and utilise the retrieved information may not have had the procedural knowledge to retrieve it in the first place.

In any organisation you will find a wide range of individual knowledge and skills. Some groups of individuals will possess deep semantic knowledge, while others possess deep procedural knowledge. The system has to accommodate both, and has to ensure that their knowledge and skills are utilised effectively.

Organisational knowledge will be shared by everyone in the organisation. Previously we examined how needs analysis should take account of the organisational environment. Consideration of organisational knowledge resources does much the same thing. It recognises that individuals possess social and cultural knowledge through their interactions with an organisational group or groups. This might include shared knowledge of departmental structure and shared knowledge of terminology – both of which can influence the structure and naming of categories in a taxonomy. For example, I know that there are four main areas within London Metropolitan University: academic departments, professional service departments, research centres and research institutes. That is organisational knowledge that is shared by everyone that works at London Met.

Lucas and Ogilvie write that organisational culture 'is an integrating mechanism that holds a diverse group of employees together. A consensus develops among members of a group because they share similar views of the world.'[19] Organisational knowledge can, of course, impact on people's willingness to share their individual knowledge. The culture may reward knowledge sharing and engender a sense of shared community, in which case information is likely to flow more freely. If people share negative perceptions about the organisation, then improving information systems is unlikely to improve information and knowledge sharing.

Acknowledgement of individual differences in terms of knowledge and skills resources can be seen in information systems which attempt to accommodate both expert and novice users for example. User-centred system design has to allow for different levels of knowledge and skills resources in the system users. This could mean having a command interface for expert users and a series of menu choices for novice users. But acknowledgement of individual differences goes far beyond differentiating between novice and expert. Designing for individual differences also has to take into account styles and preferences. I, of course, know how to use the library catalogue, but I hardly ever use it – I much prefer to just go straight to the shelves and browse even when

I am looking for a known item. That behaviour perhaps would not be predicted by knowledge of my expertise in library use.

Individual differences are often seen as synonymous with cognitive styles, which are tendencies of individuals to adopt a particular type of information processing or problem-solving strategy. There have been a number of studies examining how cognitive style can impact on both learning strategies and information-seeking strategies. This is a large area and treatment here is necessarily brief. Again, suggestions for further reading have been provided at the end of the chapter for those wishing to explore the area in more depth.

Pask[20] differentiated between holists and serialists. Holists tend to adopt a global approach to learning, examining interrelationships between several topics and concentrating first on building a broad conceptual overview before attending to specific detail. Serialists tend to examine one thing at a time, and concentrate on separate topics and the logical sequences linking them before trying to form a complete picture. This has clear implications for information architecture. The holist adopts what is a comparatively high-risk, exploratory strategy, switching attention across a range of tasks before any one is completed. The holist progresses in an exploratory fashion compared to the serialist's narrow focus and step-by-step logical progression. In the information system environment this might mean that, regardless of knowledge and skills levels, some people might just like to explore a taxonomy while others might prefer to conduct keyword searching or scan alphabetical lists. In other words, information tactics adopted by individual system users are not capable of being predicted on the basis of their individual knowledge.

Witkin[21] studied perceptual and cognitive style and, like Pask, divided people into two categories: field-dependent and field-independent. Basically, some people cannot see the trees for the wood. Field-dependent people have difficulty seeing detail and may not be able to grasp that the easiest way to solve a problem is to break it down into a series of discrete tasks. They do not necessarily perceive the complexity of a situation and have relatively poor analytic skills. It can be surmised that field-dependent users would give up a search in a taxonomy if they had not found what they were looking for after a couple of mouse clicks. Field-independent people, on the other hand, are good at structuring and analysis. They are good at defining problems and finding solutions. If a first attempt to find information was unsuccessful, field-independent users would rephrase their search statement, use different terminology, try a different path in a taxonomy. Even if their individual knowledge of a subject was limited their cognitive style would allow them to adopt relatively sophisticated problem-solving strategies to improve their understanding.

In any theory of cognitive style, the common element is that people will perceive problems differently and this will affect how they attempt to solve them. Individual differences will also impact on people's preferences in terms of screen design: layout, text size, use of colour and so on. This suggests that the interface should allow for customisation to accommodate individual preferences.

An exercise

To fully understand the complexity of the areas covered so far in this chapter, it is useful to put them into a personal context. This can be done either individually or working with a group of colleagues. Think of a simple scenario where you have needed information in the last month. This could be work related (writing a report, answering a customer query), or not (buying a new mobile phone, booking a flight). Next, break down your scenario or high-level task into a series of sub-tasks or tactics – including the less formal tactics like talking to people. As well as performing the task analysis itself also think about the individual and organisational resources you used to complete the task. If you are working with a group of colleagues you can also consider the impact of individual differences. For example, would the other members of the group have gone about satisfying the information need in the same way? Are you a holist or a serialist?

We generally do not think about our interactions with systems and other resources as we seek answers to questions or attempt to achieve some aim. This means that we may underestimate the complexity of the process and may discount system features that help us to achieve our goal.

Your task analysis should resemble Figure 2.6. This is actually an uncharacteristically quick and simple example using Amazon. Typically it would be necessary to try different search terms and look at more product details, including contents lists and some of the text of the books before placing an order. I would often check my recommendations before starting a search, assuming I had already purchased some books on the same subject or genre. Also the first time anyone uses Amazon they have to set up their password and input their address and payment details. The Amazon site is well designed and supports a range of searching and browsing tasks: the task analysis presented here looks complex but the task took less than five minutes to complete. One issue that a systems

Figure 2.6   Task analysis: buying a book

Turn on computer

Click on AOL icon

Click on Sign On button

Click in Start box

Type amazon.co.uk

Press Enter key

Click on Books

Click in Search box

Type interface design

Press Enter key

Scroll down results display

Click on book title

Scroll down page

Click on See all reviews

Scroll down page

Click on Back button

Click on Back button

Scroll down page

Click on More results

Scroll down page

Click on book title

Scroll down page

Click on Read all reviews

Scroll down page

Scroll up page

Click on Add to shopping basket

Click on Back button

Click on Back button

Click on Back button

Scroll down page

Scroll up page

Click on View basket

Figure 2.6 Task analysis: buying a book (*cont'd*)

Click on Proceed to checkout

Type password

Press Enter key

Click on Place your order

designer may want to address is the amount of scrolling up and down the page the completion of the task required – the ability to customise the amount of detail in the results display might be a useful feature.

A task that may at first seem very simple may in fact be extremely complex and resource intensive when all the associated sub-tasks are taken into consideration. Examining the range of sub-tasks and individual tactics which users adopt when they are performing an information task and using an information system highlights the complexity of the information search process.

User modelling

When you have completed the information needs analysis, identified the various tasks people perform when attempting to satisfy their information needs and analysed the resources people possess, you can then try to embody all this information in a user model or, more commonly, a set of user models.

All the behaviour we have examined so far is extremely complex; the purpose of a model is to attempt to simplify. If you have analysed the information behaviour of a group of people, and in an organisation we may be talking about hundreds of individuals, you will find that everyone is unique: with skills and knowledge unique to themselves. It is very difficult to design systems which will accommodate the very wide range of individual differences you encounter, so you have to compromise. In other words, you categorise the users; you look for similarities and create models based on those similarities. Some user modelling is essentially stereotyping, which is rather primitive, while other user modelling is quite sophisticated. Both types of modelling are examined here.

The simplest type of user modelling is a generic approach that can be applied in all information systems environments. Shneiderman, for example, separates users into:

- novice or first-time users;
- knowledgeable intermittent users;
- expert frequent users.[22]

Each type of user will have different capabilities and different needs that should be catered for by the system. Novice or first-time users will need a lot of help in reducing anxiety. Simplicity and informative feedback are important. Availability of paper manuals and online tutorials is assumed to be important. Knowledgeable intermittent users will be helped by good structure which will allow them to remember how to navigate the information store. Online help screens will allow them to check how to complete their various information tasks. Expert frequent users will appreciate short-cuts through a command interface and menus. They will want to complete their tasks as quickly and efficiently as possible.

While this type of user-modelling can be useful in suggesting the various needs that must be supported by the system interface, it does not really take account of individual differences, and is essentially stereotyping users based on the frequency of their use of an information system. It is better than no model at all, but it does not really tell you much about system users.

Another model that is often treated in the literature is the GOMS model, originated by Card et al., which attempts to model the knowledge and cognitive processes used when people interact with systems. GOMS stands for:

- Goals – what the user wants to achieve.
- Operators – cognitive processes and physical actions.
- Methods – learned procedures for accomplishing goals.
- Selection rules – which method to select when there is more than one available.[23]

The GOMS model is mentioned here because there is a lot written about it, but it is really modelling tasks not users. It essentially tries to predict what a user will do when faced with a particular task, but it does not allow for errors and it does not allow for the unpredictability of users. It oversimplifies.

You do not even have to interview and observe users to come up with these models – they apply in all cases and to all systems. We will return to this in Chapter 5, when we look at interface design and interaction styles. A much better, more sophisticated approach to user modelling, that takes account of the particular organisational environment, is to use the needs analysis to create a series of what Garrett calls 'personas',[24] as shown in Figure 2.7.

User 1 and User 2 do not actually exist, but they are representative of people within the organisation – they are models derived from the needs analysis. A problem with this approach is that you may generate too many models; in a large organisation people will perform many roles and it is not necessarily helpful to create a series of models based on those roles. You may also find that the personas you have created on the basis of role within the organisation do not explain people's use of the information systems and services: the personas model needs (and their related tasks) rather than users. This is a very good starting point – see the case study below – but provides only a partial picture. In terms of their use of an information system, Users 1 and 2, although accessing different things, may exhibit almost identical behaviour. The most useful models will not focus on level of expertise, tasks or organisational role, but will concentrate on search behaviour.

Another way to approach user-modelling is to analyse actual use of an existing or prototype system. Observing people using an organisation's existing information system can help to identify, first of all, how it is used

Figure 2.7	Personas

User 1 works in research and publishes regular papers about current projects on the organisation's intranet as well as writing for scholarly and trade journals. He or she needs frequent access to:

- external sources of information;

- research and development budgets;

- the organisation's metadata template;

- publishing software.

User 2 works in sales and is in close contact with the organisation's customers. He or she needs frequent access to:

- product information;

- customer accounts;

- spreadsheet software.

and, secondly, how it could be improved. Observation of this kind should result in the creation of more sophisticated, context-specific user models that take account of individual preferences. This type of modelling is explained in more detail in the summary below.

At this point it should be stated that, no matter how sophisticated your user models, there is a danger in attempting to simplify complex behaviour. As noted previously, it is essential to categorise users in some way because it is not going to be possible to design systems accommodating the complete range of behaviours you will encounter. On the other hand your models should not be used to restrict the flexibility of systems. Individual users should be able to customise their interactions to some extent. Models can suggest basic system functionality but the system should allow individual users to adopt their preferred interaction styles.

Summary: a case study

It is useful to summarise what we have covered in this chapter by putting it into the context of the whole design process. What follows is a personal narrative of information system design. The context, the purpose of the research, was to determine how people searched for images in a picture database. A picture database of photographs by nineteenth-century Scottish photographer George Washington Wilson was created and retrieval software was developed to allow users to search and browse the database for images.

The first point to make is that the search behaviour of an individual will be, to a greater or lesser extent, determined by the nature of their information need. Experienced users will adopt different strategies depending on whether they are seeking a known item or simply looking for everything on a particular subject, for example. So maybe the first thing to do, based on the information needs analysis discussed in the first section of this chapter, is to create categories or models of information need, before attempting to create user models.

The first step in creating a search and retrieval system for a database of photographs of nineteenth-century Scotland was to analyse and then categorise visual information needs. Four categories seemed to encompass the whole range of pictorial information needs – these became representative tasks:

1. *Specific nameable*: the Scott Monument in Edinburgh, the River Dee.
2. *General nameable*: a ruined castle, a tram.

3. *Abstract*: a busy street scene, an arch shape.

4. *Subjective*: a pretty picture, a scene that shows how times have changed.

Having analysed and categorised the information resource and its associated needs to identify a series of representative tasks, the next step was to find out what search tasks or tactics people performed when attempting to satisfy the different types of need. In theory, and in very simple terms, some of the above needs (specific and general nameable) could be best satisfied by querying by keyword to retrieve a small set of pictures matching the terms input to the system; others (abstract and subjective) could be best satisfied by browsing which would expose users to larger sets of images which they could then compare and contrast before deciding which image or images best matched their requirements. It was rather naively assumed that the majority of users would adopt tactics that best suited the task at hand.

To test a prototype retrieval system, diverse groups of people were used: people who would have different levels of knowledge, of nineteenth-century Scotland in this case, and different levels of skills in terms of information search and experience with computers:

1. Historians

2. Professional librarians

3. Master of Education students

4. Postgraduate and undergraduate librarianship students

5. Schoolchildren (12–17 years).

The groups can be likened to the personas mentioned in the section on user modelling. Each group brought different resources in terms of levels of knowledge and aptitude to the search process. The original hypothesis was that membership of a group would bring with it definable knowledge and skills that could be used to predict search behaviour. People in different groups would have different preferences as to how they conducted their searches. People with extensive subject knowledge and/or information retrieval skills would prefer a combination of keyword searching and browsing. People with limited subject knowledge and/or experience of information retrieval would prefer keyword searching. Schoolchildren, it was assumed, would have relatively unsophisticated analytical skills and would prefer to browse the images.

Having conducted what was essentially a needs and resource analysis, the next step was to design a prototype system which would allow people to satisfy the different types of needs while utilising their preferred search type. The system incorporated three types of search:

1. *Keyword search*: using single words and simple phrases.

2. *Menu-based browsing*: eight top-level categories provided access to a structured browsing environment: Aberdeen, Castles, Cathedrals, Edinburgh, Fishing Industry, Lochs, Mountains, Rivers.

3. *Scanning*: a joystick was used to control speed and direction when scanning the images in the database, from one picture per second to fifty pictures per second.

The system utilised analogue technology (laserdisc); digital technologies would have allowed for a wider range of browsing options, for example thumbnail images to compare and contrast on a single screen.

The next step was to find out what tactics people used when attempting to complete the different types of task or satisfy the different types of need. Users were asked to search for images representing the various needs or tasks outlined above. People were asked to talk through what they were doing as they were using the retrieval system to complete the various tasks, and they were videoed so that the data could be analysed at a later time. The system itself was automatically creating a log of all their interactions with it, generating quantitative data as well as qualitative. The quantitative data was useful in creating a series of user models and the qualitative data was useful in redesigning the interface to the system to make it more user-centred: users were talking about what they would like to be able to do in addition to what they could do, mentioning features of the system they liked and disliked, and so on. The task analysis was crucial in that it fed directly into making the system more user-centred.

Based on use of the information system by people within the various user groups, categories of search behaviour were created. These became user models which were applied to the next stage of the design process, assisting in refining the system to make it more user-centred. In almost every case search behaviour, and its associated user model, could not be predicted by membership in one of the original user groups – the only exception were the undergraduate librarianship students who wanted to use keyword searching for everything because they had been trained to believe that that was the only way you should search for information.

Users fell into one of four groups:

1. Excluders

2. Focusers

3. Explorers

4. Wanderers.

While not wanting to encourage the excluders and the wanderers, the picture information retrieval system incorporated search features that would accommodate each type of user. Excluders used keyword only and tended to settle for the first image they retrieved. Focusers used keyword search or menu browsing and examined a relatively small group of images before deciding on the image or images which best met their requirements. Explorers used keyword search, menu browsing or scanning and examined many images before reaching their decision. (This was the category which showed the richest variety of behaviour and it could have been broken down further.) Wanderers used scanning and went all over the place, backwards and forwards, sometimes looking at the same groups of images many times in their wanderings.

The point is that, to design a picture retrieval system that was truly user-centred, it was necessary to design for all four types of user. It was simpler to do that based on the user models that had been created than to attempt to accommodate the whole range of individual differences. That is the strength of user modelling; the drawback is that you can end up oversimplifying.

This case study has demonstrated how needs analysis, task analysis, resource analysis and user modelling all feed into user-centred systems design. If you do not know what information users of the system need access to, then important content may be omitted. If you do not know what tasks users perform as they search for information, then important functionality may be omitted or, as Norman warns, you overwhelm the system with useless functionality. If you do not know how users prefer to interact with the system then features that would cater for individual differences may be omitted; if we bear in mind Kuhlthau's affect realm this may have a significant effect on system use. If you do not try to simplify all the data you generate during the information audit, then you will be drowning in complexity and you will probably end up buying a generic software solution that does not address specific organisational needs.

A final personal aside. A few years ago a student attended a three-day short course I was running on taxonomy creation. Their employer wanted them to complete the course and then go into work and 'do' a taxonomy, assuming it would take a few days or, at worst, a few weeks – the structuring would be easy, programming and adding content might take some time. It is depressingly easy to identify websites where no thought has gone into needs, tasks and preferences. The preliminaries are time-consuming and expensive but the investment is worth it.

Further reading

Several books and papers listed in the references have good coverage of the aspects of systems design discussed and explained in this chapter. Recommended for basic reading are the following:

A good introduction to the concepts of needs, task and resource analysis:

- Allen, B. (1996) *Information Tasks: Toward a User-Centered Approach to Information Systems*. London: Academic Press.

Research methods were dealt with only superficially in the text. The following represent good, basic introductions to methodologies and methods:

- Dawson, C. (2006) *A Practical Guide to Research Methods*, 2nd edn. Oxford: How To Books.
- Flick, U. (2006) *An Introduction to Qualitative Research*, 3rd edn. London: Sage.
- Gorman, G.E. and Clayton, P. (2005) *Qualitative Research for the Information Professional*. London: Facet.
- Oppenheim, A.N. (2000) *Questionnaire Design, Interviewing and Attitude Measurement*, new edn. London: Continuum.

A good overview of the work of Pask and Witkin on cognitive styles in the context of information seeking:

- Ford, N.J. et al. (1999) 'Cognitive styles in information seeking analysis', in T.D. Wilson et al. (eds), *Uncertainty in Information Seeking*, at: *http://informationr.net/tdw/publ/unis/app7.4.html* (accessed 18 July 2006).

References

1. Dubois, C.P.R. (1995) 'The information audit: its contribution to decision making', *Library Management*, 16 (7): 20–4.

2. TFPL, *Information and Knowledge Audits*, *http://www.tfpl .com/advice/km/km_audits.cfm* (accessed 18 July 2006).

3. Evernden, R. and Evernden, E. (2003) *Information First: Integrating Knowledge and Information Architecture for Business Advantage.* Oxford: Elsevier, p. 96.

4. Rodenberg & Tillman Associates: *http://www.rodenberg.nl/ information_audit.html* (accessed 18 July 2006).

5. Line, M.B. (1974) 'Draft definitions: information and library needs, wants, demands and uses', *Aslib Proceedings*, 26 (2): 87.

6. Taylor, R.S. (1968) 'Question negotiation and information seeking in libraries', *College and Research Libraries*, 29: 178–94.

7. Belkin, N.J. et al. (1982) 'ASK for information retrieval: Part I', *Journal of Documentation*, 38 (2): 61–71.

8. Rohde, N.F. (1986) 'Information needs', *Advances in Librarianship*, Vol. 14. London: Academic Press, pp. 49–73.

9. Attwood, R. and Dervin, B. (1981) 'Challenges to sociocultural predictors of information seeking', in M. Burgoon (ed.), *Communication Yearbook 5*. Piscataway, NJ: Transaction Press, pp. 549–69.

10. Wilson, T.D. and Streatfield, D.R. (1977) 'Information needs in local authority social services departments: an interim report on Project INISS', *Journal of Documentation*, 33 (4): 277–93.

11. Wilson, T.D. et al. (1979) 'Information needs in local authority social services departments: a second report on Project INISS', *Journal of Documentation*, 35 (2): 120–36.

12. Ibid.

13. TFPL, op. cit.

14. Marshall, C. et al. (1987) 'Design guidelines', in M.M. Gardiner and B. Christie (eds), *Applying Cognitive Psychology to User Interface Design*. Chichester: Wiley.

15. Norman, D.A. (2004) *Emotional Design: Why We Love (or Hate) Everyday Things*. New York: Basic Books, p. 71.

16. Allen, B. (1996) *Information Tasks: Toward a User-Centered Approach to Information Systems*. London: Academic Press, pp. 49–50.

17. Kuhlthau, C.C. (1993) *Seeking Meaning: A Process Approach to Library and Information Systems*. Norwood, NJ: Ablex, pp. 41–2.

18. Marchionini, G. (1992) 'Interfaces for end-user information seeking', *Journal of the American Society for Information Science*, 43 (2): 156–63.

19. Lucas, L.M. and Ogilvie, D.T. (2006) 'Things are not always what they seem: how reputations, culture and incentives influence knowledge transfer', *The Learning Organization*, 13 (1): 7–24.
20. Pask, G. (1976) 'Styles and strategies of learning', *British Journal of Educational Psychology*, 46: 128–48.
21. Witkin, H.A. et al. (1977) 'Field-dependent and field-independent cognitive styles and their educational implications', *Review of Educational Research*, 47: 1–64.
22. Shneiderman, B. (2004) *Designing the User Interface: Strategies for Effective Human–Computer Interaction*, 4th edn. Boston: Addison-Wesley.
23. Card, S. et al. (1983) *The Psychology of Human-Computer Interaction*. Hillsdale, NJ: Erlbaum.
24. Garrett, J.J. (2003) *The Elements of User Experience: User-Centered Design for the Web*. Indianapolis, IN: New Riders, p. 54.

Searching and finding

In this chapter the focus is on information search and retrieval. The information architecture should allow for two basic approaches to information retrieval: searching, providing a search engine to process typed queries; and finding, providing a structured browsing environment for users to explore. Both approaches will be examined here in an analysis of search engine features and taxonomy creation. The chapter is divided into two main sections:

- *Searching*: focusing on the search features that should be supported by a search engine. Here we also look at constructing search statements to increase the efficiency and precision of known-item and subject searching.

- *Finding*: looking at browsing or foraging strategies. Browsing is dependent upon structure; classification schemes like Dewey Decimal provide the type of hierarchical structure that promotes browsing in libraries. These concepts can be directly transferred to the digital environment and applied in taxonomy creation. The focus in this section is upon structuring an organisation's taxonomy to increase the efficiency of information finding.

We begin by looking at the development of a search strategy and associated searching and browsing tactics.

Search strategies

A search strategy is comprised of all the actions taken to complete an information search. Those individual actions are search tactics, which can, of course be mapped onto the search tasks we looked at in Chapter 2. You were introduced to Kuhlthau's model of the search process in that chapter, when her three realms – affective, cognitive and physical – were described. She suggests that the development and completion of an information search involves six stages: task initiation, topic selection, pre-focus exploration, focus formulation, information collection and search closure.[1] At each stage of the search the user will adopt a range of tactics and use a range of information sources. Their search strategy will evolve and develop as they progress through the various stages. Sources used may include colleagues, reference works, a library or other information store and internal and external information systems. Tactics used may include discussion, data checking, analytical (keyword) searching and browsing. Search closure is reached when the needed information has been found and the information task can be completed: a fact verified, a customer query answered or a report written, for example.

We have already seen, in the section on task analysis, that the behaviour we engage in when searching for information is extremely complex. Bates termed this behaviour 'berrypicking',[2] and noted that the searcher who can apply the widest range of search strategies is the searcher with the greatest retrieval power. There are two assumptions here: that the searcher has the requisite skills – is able to adapt their search technique to meet the demands of the task; and that the system can support the various strategies adopted by the searcher. Bates's berrypicking model incorporates both analytical and browsing tactics; she suggests that users will move seamlessly from one technique to the other, assuming the system allows them to do so.

Searching strategies

Searching is here taken to mean keyword searching, sometimes termed analytical searching.[3] In the context of information architecture and systems' development in organisations, this type of searching is supported by the provision of a search engine that allows users to input and modify queries in the form of simple keywords and more complicated search statements. The search features that ought to be present are examined in detail in the following section on search features and search statements; here we concentrate on the broader strategy. In Chapter 1 the concepts of pre- and post-coordinate indexes were described; keyword searching is reliant on post-coordination: the user combines index terms when they type a phrase or a formal search statement in the search box. The success of the search depends on the user's skill and experience in selecting and combining terms and in responding to feedback from the system (in the form of results) to modify their search statement. Most users will type a single word or simple phrase when interrogating a search engine or other information system. This is hardly a systematic or analytical strategy, but assuming the word or phrase used to query the system adequately represents the problem, then the user may be satisfied with the results and reaches search closure.

Harter[4] describes a 'building blocks' approach to searching in information systems. Here the user begins by identifying the main concepts associated with their information need; these become the basis of their searching activities. Having queried the system and scanned the results, the user would build upon their original problem statement by adding more terms or by combining terms in different ways to narrow or broaden their search and increase or decrease the number of items retrieved. Another analytical strategy is the 'pearl-growing' approach.[5] This depends upon the searcher having one relevant item and using it as the basis for further searching: using it to identify more key terms, following up items in its list of references, searching a citation index to find other articles that have cited the original item. All of these strategies are dependent on the quality of the feedback from the system and the user's ability to interact with it as they develop their query.

Browsing strategies

Browsing is often assumed to be a rather untidy, purely random activity, but from the early 1970s there has been interest in browsing as a valid alternative to keyword searching, with writers like Salton,[6] Hildreth,[7] and Palay and Fox[8] suggesting that information systems would benefit from support for browsing. Perhaps the problem with the concept lies in its name, with browsing being historically associated with the physical library environment, as in Hildreth's description:

> Undoubtedly, the most visible and commonly understood browsing activity is the roaming among the shelf areas of a library or bookstore to scan materials of potential interest. Books are casually perused in order to decide what we want to buy or borrow, if anything at all.[9]

This certainly describes one type of browsing behaviour, but by no means all types. A better term to describe the range of behaviours associated with browsing may be 'foraging', a term increasingly used in the literature and suggesting a much more purposeful activity. It is possible to identify at least three types of browsing or foraging: widely exploratory, serendipitous browsing; purposeful browsing, initiated by a need for information on a particular subject; and focused browsing, often concentrated on particular sources known to be useful.

Meadow describes browsing activities in the library context:

> In using a card catalogue or in scanning shelves of books, we commonly employ a complex strategy called browsing. We enter this process with a general idea of the subject of the search or even with a few very specific descriptors – perhaps title or author. If we find just what we want on the basis of the original 'query', the procedure ends. If not, we are likely to begin to search for alternative spellings, variants of subject heading terms, or different classifications under which our subject may have been classified. The routine proceeds so smoothly and informally that we may not recognise its basic nature.[10]

He raises several important points here: he is describing a systematic search process; he suggests that browsing is a comfortable and natural way to search for information; and he touches on the value of browsing as a means of expanding and extending a search for information – one of the main values of browsing as a way of searching for information is that it allows users to broaden their sphere of interest. It is also easy to transfer the behaviour he describes into the information systems environment. In fact the behaviour he describes is very like the berrypicking strategy described by Bates, incorporating a range of activities from the analytical to the almost serendipitous.

We know that libraries organise for browsing: classification schemes provide a subject arrangement of books on shelves: subject groupings help browsers because they can identify which part of the library to browse in. Information systems can also organise for browsing: web directories, for example, provide a browsing environment. Menus can be used to create hierarchies, guiding the user through a series of choices to increasingly specific information.

Summary

A search strategy is unlikely to consist solely of analytical or browsing tactics (see Figure 3.1), although the user will initiate the process by

Figure 3.1 Features of searching and browsing

Searching
      Attribute:Exclusivity
      Need: Specific
      Activities: Narrowing
                         Focusing

Browsing
      Attribute:Exploration
      Need: Specific
                         Vague
                         Changing
      Activities: Exploring
                         Scanning
                         Extending

adopting one or the other type of search. As the user queries the system by typing terms in a search box, or selects a category in a taxonomy, scans results, modifies their query and follows links to other potentially useful items, they shift seamlessly from one type of tactic to another. The challenge for information architects is to support the many different ways in which users will interact with a system by providing powerful search and browsing tools, and ensuring that the system interface allows the strategy to develop naturally. Ideally the user should be unaware of the complexity of the process they are engaging in.

Search features and search statements

In this section we concentrate on the search engine: telling the system what it is we are actually looking for. Very simplistically, this involves entering search terms, combining them in various ways, and reading, printing or downloading results. This may, in fact, be a very simple process. Perhaps we want information on environmental law, so we type 'environmental law'. The feedback from the system tells us that ten records match our search, and when we click on the hyperlink of the first record in the results display, we find that it is exactly what we want. Ideally this is what we would like to happen, but it is, of course, very unlikely, unless the system has very limited coverage of our subject in which case we need to search somewhere else. The feedback from the system is much more likely to tell us that 20,000 records match our request (in fact, at the time of writing, 278,000,000 on Google[11]) at which point we will probably look at the first two or three records in the results display, and if we do not find the information we need we will either give up or we will modify our search statement by, in this case, adding a term or terms to specify which aspect of environmental law we want information on.

What we actually want information on is UK environmental law on the disposal of hazardous substances. So we would modify the search by adding terms like 'hazardous substances' and 'disposal' to the original query. This process, of modifying the query in response to feedback from the system, continues until we have retrieved a set of records (perhaps one, perhaps fifty, depending on what we want the information for) which contain information, not just on environmental law, but on UK environmental law on the disposal of hazardous substances.

The success of this interaction depends on two factors: the ability of the user to modify their query and the ability of the search engine to process their query. Users can develop skills in searching so that they interrogate the system more efficiently. The search engine can offer a range of features that assist all users, novice and expert, in searching the information system.

A successful information search starts with the user knowing what it is they are looking for. The system can only respond to user queries – it will search for whatever the user asks for; so the first step in conducting an information search is selecting the terms to input. It has already been noted in the section on information needs in Chapter 2 that it is often difficult to express what information is needed: the user may not have the understanding or vocabulary to do so. The complexity of the problem can be illustrated by looking at the environmental law example in more depth.

There are many more terms that could be added to the lists in Figure 3.2. There will be, inevitably, several different ways to describe what, at first sight, appears to be a relatively straightforward subject query. The first thing to note is that if a thesaurus is available it can be consulted to check terminology and to identify broader, narrower and related terms. If the system incorporates an ontology or classic thesaurus (see Chapter 4) then user queries can be automatically expanded and mapped onto associated concepts.

The focus of this book is upon an organisation's information system and, arguably, there should be fewer problems in searching a specialised

Figure 3.2   Disposal of hazardous substances

Disposal:
    Clean-up
    Contamination
    Dumping
    Handling
    Landfill
    Management
    Movement
    Pollution
    Regulation
    Storage
    Transport
    Treatment

Hazardous substances:
    Asbestos
    Biohazard
    Chemical waste
    Contaminants
    Domestic waste
    Electrical equipment
    Hazardous waste
    Nuclear waste
    Oil
    Pesticides
    Radioactive waste
    Special waste
    Toxic waste
    Waste

resource. If the resource is effectively managed, then the terminology used to describe resources should be shared by all potential users of the system and consistently applied in describing those resources. In searching within a commercial system like Dialog or in searching the web with a search engine like Google, users can expect to meet wide variations in how terminology is applied, including variants in spelling; this will compound the problems associated with expressing information needs in a search statement and emphasises the importance of thinking carefully about key terms.

A search for information on a specific topic will often require the user to input different combinations of key terms, responding to feedback from the system, before the needed information is retrieved. This involves using various techniques to narrow or broaden the scope of the search. There are three basic techniques that can be applied to increase the efficiency of searching:

- *how to combine terms*: search logic, phrase, proximity;
- *how to modify single terms*: wildcards, truncation;
- *how to restrict the scope of the search*: fields, limits.

Combining terms

Terms can be combined using search logic. The earliest online retrieval systems, developed in the 1960s, introduced the use of the logical operators AND, OR, NOT, originally formulated by the nineteenth-century mathematician George Boole and consequently called Boolean operators. Current systems support full and/or implied Boolean searching to increase the precision of retrieval. Generally, if full Boolean is supported, the operators have to be capitalised to distinguish them from common words.

AND is used to link different concepts of a search. This narrows the scope of the search and results in fewer items being retrieved:

hazardous AND substances AND disposal

Only items that contain all three terms will be retrieved. Most search engines will apply the Boolean AND by default so it does not need to be included in the search statement. This cannot be taken for granted though: some search engines may apply the Boolean OR (see below) by default which would completely change the results of the search. In some search engines the Boolean AND is expressed as a plus sign:

+hazardous +substances +disposal

This is typically the case in the simple search offerings of the major search engines – the plus sign can be used, for example, to force the system to search for stop words. Stop words are common words that you would expect to find in most documents and so they are generally excluded from the search, either because they are not indexed in the first place or because they would increase the time taken to process the search. The system simply ignores words like the, of, by, and, for, with, from, to, and so on, unless specifically instructed to include them in the search.

OR is used to link related concepts of a search; it broadens the scope of the search rather than narrowing it. OR is very useful for synonyms:

hazardous AND (waste OR substances) AND (disposal OR management)

In this example the OR statements have been nested: enclosed within parentheses. It is important to do this because systems will typically process the AND statement first; parentheses are used to force the system to process the OR statement first. A simpler example to illustrate this would be:

hazardous AND waste OR substances

Without parentheses the system would typically search for items that contain both 'hazardous' and 'waste' and then to the results of that search add all the items containing the term 'substances'. By enclosing the OR statement in parentheses the system searches for all items containing the terms 'hazardous' and 'waste' and all the items containing the terms 'hazardous' and 'substances'.

NOT is used to exclude concepts from a search:

hazardous AND (waste OR substances) AND (disposal OR management) NOT radioactive

Any records that contain the term 'radioactive' are excluded. Search engines will typically recognise the minus sign (–) as the Boolean NOT operator. This is a very effective way to narrow the results of a search, although there is a danger that potentially relevant items may be missed if they contain the excluded term.

Most of the major search engines support the AND and NOT operators, often expressed as plus and minus, in their simple search and, as noted above, most will apply the Boolean AND as default in compiling their results. In advanced search mode the user is generally presented with options to search for 'All the words' (AND), 'Any of the words' or 'At least one of the words' (OR) and 'Without the words' (NOT). Many do not allow the user to construct full Boolean search statements, which may be a disadvantage for expert users.

The search engine should be able to conduct phrase searches. Most systems will rank their results in a way that items with query terms adjacent to each other will be at the top of the results display, or they will automatically search for phrases. Simply typing hazardous substances in the search box should retrieve items that not only contain both terms but contain them as a phrase. It is also usually possible to force phrase searching by enclosing the phrase in quotation marks: "hazardous substances" or by using the 'With the exact phrase' search box in advanced search mode. Support for phrase searching is essential as this will hugely increase the precision of retrieval.

Arguably less important, and less common, than phrase searching is to allow for terms to be combined with proximity operators. The problem with phrase searching is that items have to include the phrase as enclosed in quotation marks, and the problem with combining terms with the Boolean AND is that the items retrieved may contain all the terms in the query but not in the required context. In Figures 3.3 and 3.4 simple rephrasing of the search statement has a significant impact on the results, including, crucially, if the user selected Google's 'I'm feeling lucky' button, the top result.

If we used the Boolean AND to combine terms this would simply instruct the system to find items that include the three words hazardous and substances and disposal. This may result in the retrieval of records that include phrases like: 'controlled substances', 'hazardous to health', 'needle disposal'. All the terms are present in the item but not in the expected context. Using proximity operators, you can specify that terms must appear within a certain number of words from each other. Support for proximity searching is difficult to find in web search engines. Alta Vista[12] used to support the NEAR operator to specify that terms had to appear within ten words of each other, but this feature seems to have been dropped. Exalead[13] appears to be the only general search engine now offering proximity searching: terms must be within 16 words of each other. In contrast to this, Dialog has very sophisticated proximity searching facilities, using the letter W or the letter N plus, where necessary, a number in brackets.

In Figure 3.5, the first line of the results (S1) demonstrates that Dialog does not support simple phrase searching: terms in phrases (unless they are compound headings used as formal subject descriptors) have to be joined by the (w) operator. The next three lines (S2, S3 and S4) show the number of items in the database containing each of the individual terms. In the final line of the results (S5) hazardous(w)substance specifies that the two terms must be adjacent to each other and in the order specified; (6n)disposal means that the term must appear within 6 words of 'hazardous substances', either preceding or following. So that search

Figure 3.3 Search for 'hazardous substances disposal'

Source: www.google.co.uk

Figure 3.4 Search for 'disposal of hazardous substances'

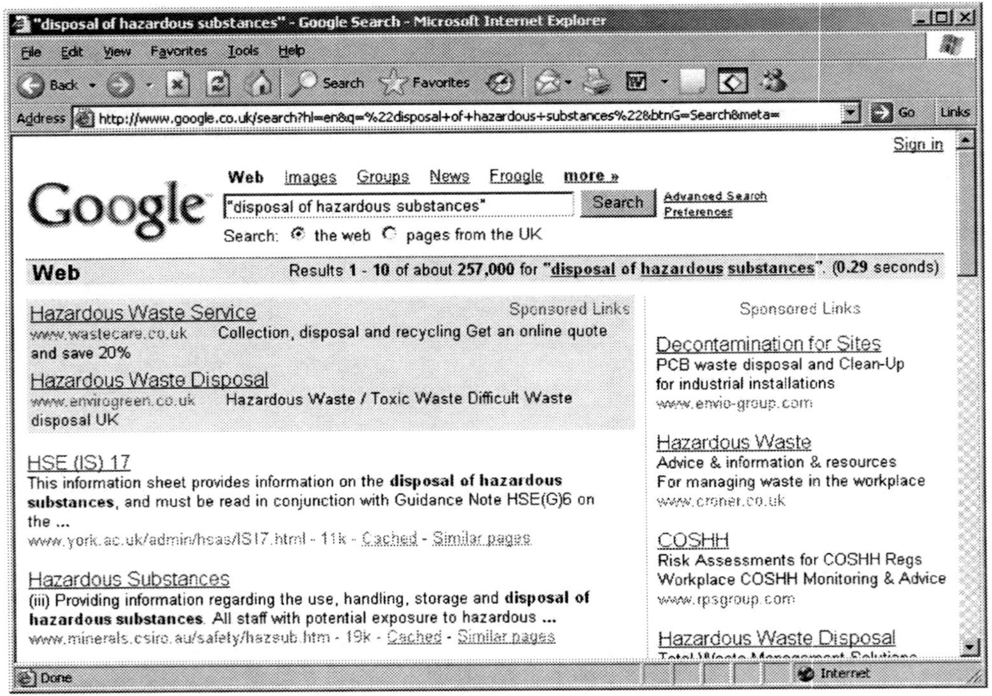

Source: www.google.co.uk

Figure 3.5 Dialog search

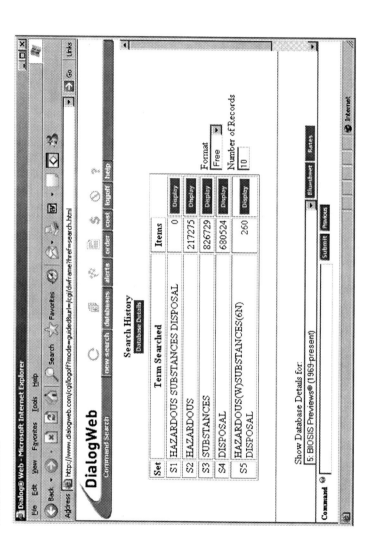

statement has retrieved items including, for example: 'disposal of hazardous substances', 'disposal facilities for the management of hazardous substances', 'hazardous substances and their disposal'. Using proximity operators carefully, the scope of the search can be broadened without the risk of retrieving a lot of irrelevant items.

Modifying terms

The second basic search feature that needs to be explained is how to modify single terms when interrogating a database. Remember that most information retrieval systems are basically stupid: they do not infer meaning; they retrieve exactly what they are asked to retrieve. So if a user types 'toxic' that is what the system looks for – it will not retrieve records that include the terms toxin, toxins or toxicity. If a user types 'organisation', the system will not retrieve records that include organise, organising or the variant spelling with 'z' rather than 's'. To ensure that all the relevant records are retrieved truncation or word stemming can be used. Different systems use different symbols; in Dialog open truncation is achieved using a single question mark: 'toxi?' would retrieve: toxic, toxin, toxins, toxicity, toxical, toxication, toxicology and so on – all words that begin with the letters 'toxi'. A question mark is also used as a wildcard to replace single characters within words: organi?ation would retrieve both organisation and organization. Carefully used, truncation allows you broaden the scope of your search while ensuring only relevant records are retrieved.

Dialog has very sophisticated truncation features: open and internal truncation as described above, and restricted truncation. Using two question marks with an intervening space instructs the system to search for a maximum of one additional character after the stem: 'toxi? ?' would retrieve toxic or toxin. It is also possible to specify the maximum number of additional characters after the stem using several question marks with no intervening spaces: 'toxi??' would retrieve toxic, toxin, toxins.

This level of control is not found in search engines – most do not offer truncation features. Northern Light,[14] no longer a free search engine, offered the most powerful features, with internal, open and restricted truncation. Some search engines (for example Google and Exalead) offer automatic word stemming and will automatically search for plurals and variants of words. In the absence of any other support for truncation this is an essential feature and will save the user considerable time and effort. Google also offers a synonym search using the tilde symbol (~) which can replace truncation features to some extent by looking for variants of words.

Fields and limits

The final basic search technique to be described is the use of fields and limits. It is very useful to be able to restrict a search to a particular field in a record and to limit results by language and date, for example. Every record in a database contains a number of separate fields: author field, title field, subject field, language field, date field and so on (see also the section on metadata for further coverage of fields). Ideally each field would be capable of being searched separately, or a field search could be included as part of a general query. All major search engines include fields and limits to increase the precision of search results. For example, the 'Occurrences' option in the Google Advanced Search (see Figure 3.6) allows users to specify that their terms must appear in the URL, in the title, in a designated website, and so on. Limits are available for language, date, file type (HTML, PDF, etc.) and domain (.com, .gov, etc.).

Many of the databases hosted by Dialog, as may be expected, have very sophisticated field structures and limits that can be used to increase the precision of retrieval. Specific fields and their codes can vary from database to database, so it is always advisable to check the database details in the Bluesheets before commencing a search. The example in Figure 3.7 shows some of the searchable fields in the Inspec database and gives an indication of the depth of detail achieved. Dialog Bluesheets are not password protected and can be accessed at: *http://www.dialog.com/ bluesheets/*.

Fields and limits are obviously used to narrow the scope of a search. If a search of the complete set of records in the database results in a large number of items being retrieved, and if you cannot think of any way to add terms to make the search statement more specific, then you can narrow the search, and make sure that the topic you are interested in is the central topic of the retrieved records by limiting the search to the title field, or lead paragraph, or title and abstract. For example, in Dialog:

hazardous(w)substances/TI
hazardous(w)substances/LP
hazardous(w)substances/TI,AB.

A useful way to limit a search is to ask for only information published in, for example, the past two years. Again, Dialog allows for a lot of sophistication:

py>2004 (published after 2004)
py=2005:2006 (published in those two years)
py=2006 (published in that year)

Figure 3.6   Google Advanced Search

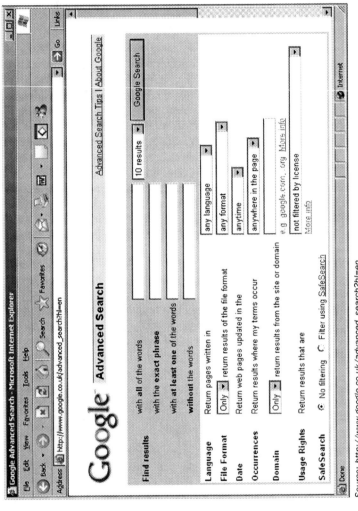

Source: http://www.google.co.uk/advanced_search?hl=en

Figure 3.7   Dialog Bluesheets: some of the searchable fields in the Inspec database

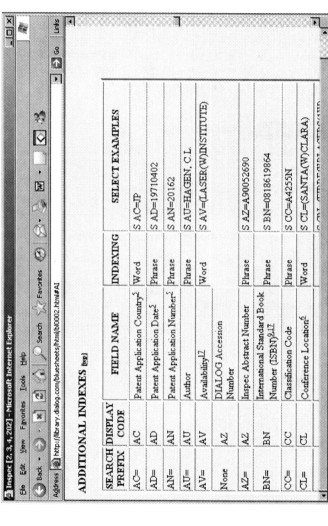

Most search engines have date limits of 'anytime', 'past three months', 'past six months' and 'past year'.

Summary

Search engines do not offer the sophisticated range of search features offered by a legacy host like Dialog, but such sophistication would be unnecessary for the majority of users within the organisation anyway. There are, however, various features that are particularly desirable and which should be present (see Figure 3.8).

Figure 3.8 Search features

Boolean

- Default AND to combine search terms

- Support for NOT (–) to exclude terms

- Support for OR for synonyms and variant spellings

- Support for full Boolean searching is desirable but not essential

Phrase

- Essential to increase efficiency

Proximity

- Desirable but not essential

Truncation

- Desirable but not essential

Word stemming

- Automatic plurals searching is essential

Fields

- Author, title, subject at least

Limits

- Date and file type at least

Support for these features in major search engines is variable (see, for example, the Search Engine Showdown features chart[15]) but it is suggested that when selecting the application to power an organisation's search engine, the essential features outlined should be present to increase the efficiency of search and retrieval and to accommodate both expert and novice searchers. Ideally the system's search engine should support the whole range of features discussed in this section, but being pragmatic, some features are more important than others. The task analysis as discussed in Chapter 2 will suggest the functionality the system users will require.

Finding

In this section the focus is on a taxonomy as a browsing tool which system users can explore to find, rather than search for, wanted items. In developing a search strategy users will employ a range of tactics, switching as seamlessly as the system will allow between searching and browsing. In our consideration of resources in Chapter 2 we explored how individual preferences can impact upon the ways in which people interact with an information system. To accommodate the full range of individual resources and information-seeking tactics a taxonomy or subject tree must be provided. In Chapter 1 the basic principles of classification were outlined – a more in-depth treatment is required here. Before we can develop an understanding of organising or classifying resources in the digital environment, we need to understand classification theory and traditional library classification. Taxonomies in the digital environment owe a great deal to principles of classification as exemplified in classification schemes like Dewey Decimal. One concept that translates directly from library classification to taxonomies is expressiveness – explicit display of hierarchies. Another concept that is of vital importance is that of hospitality – the ability to accommodate new concepts or subject areas. In this section the initial focus is on basic theories of classification, examining enumerative and faceted classification schemes, before explaining how their principles are used in taxonomy creation.

Library classification

As an introduction to taxonomies it is useful to explore the more familiar principles of library classification schemes. This may not seem to be immediately relevant, but a taxonomy is simply a classification scheme and an understanding of taxonomy in information architecture can be facilitated by a grasp of how traditional schemes represent knowledge structures; we can learn from their mistakes and we can learn from their good points. As noted above, two features of library classification schemes are of particular relevance: hospitality – the ability to accommodate new subjects; and expressiveness – display of hierarchy. These concepts will be described and discussed further in the context of specific classification schemes.

Library classification schemes can be either enumerative or faceted. Enumerative schemes attempt to list all subjects, simple and compound. The enumeration or listing is usually achieved, first of all, by identifying the main disciplines to be covered by the scheme; these main disciplines become the main classes, then each discipline is divided into subclasses. The subdivision continues until an appropriate level of specificity has been reached, with all subjects listed in their appropriate places. In enumerative classification schemes like Library of Congress and Dewey Decimal the aim is to find one place in the listing for each subject. A strictly enumerative scheme does not allow for any joining together of concepts that have been divided from one another. When classifying a book that is multidisciplinary, a decision has to be made as to which of its subjects it will be classified under, using knowledge of the library's users to decide on the best place for the book. An example may be a book about the use of psychological testing in the selection of employees: is it classified in Psychology (in DDC in the 150s) or in management (in the 658s)? The book can only go in one place in the linear sequence and in this example it can go near the start of the sequence or near the end. In taxonomy creation the decision-making process is simpler; links can be created to a single electronic document from several points in the subject tree.

Apart from the difficulty of providing a comprehensive list of all subjects both simple and compound, an obvious problem with enumerative schemes is that subjects change and new subjects emerge that could not have been anticipated when the scheme was created. It is very difficult to reflect changing relationships between subjects and to place each new subject in its proper position among the existing subjects.

Library of Congress Classification is the clearest example of an enumerative classification scheme. An outline of the schedules is available on the Library of Congress website.[16] It is often assumed that an enumerative scheme, particularly one that lists concepts to the level of detail achieved in LCC, will have problems accommodating new topics. LCC utilises a very pragmatic approach in solving this problem: it does not have a hierarchical structure and does not aim for a helpful order of subjects, so new topics can be added very easily without compromising the overall structure of the scheme. In taxonomy this approach would not work: users need concepts to be organised in some way (logical, sequential or alphabetical) to provide the kind of structure essential to browsing.

Dewey Decimal is another example of an enumerative classification scheme but it also has features associated with faceted classification: as well as its main listing of subjects it includes tables of common concepts like geographic area that can be added to subjects in the main listing. DDC is basically arranged into 10 main classes, 100 divisions and 1,000 sections, then subdivision continues within sections until the most specific subject level is reached. So DDC has a very rigidly structured hierarchy and actually has a great deal in common with taxonomies or subject trees. Information about the scheme can be found via the Online Computer Library Center (OCLC) website.[17]

There are three ways in which DDC achieves hospitality, the ability to accommodate new subjects:

- decimal notation;
- gaps in the subject listing;
- 'other' classes.

A new subject can be fitted almost anywhere in a sequence by using decimal subdivision. For example:

600	Technology
620	Engineering
621	Applied physics
621.3	Electrical, magnetic, optical, communications, computer engineering; electronics, lighting
621.38	Electronics, communications engineering
621.388	Television
621.38833	Video recorders and video recordings

New subjects are accommodated, but parts of the Dewey hierarchy are very deep. This approach would not work in a taxonomy: assuming 'Technology' was at the top level, the user would be required to click on six category names before finding the 'Video recorders and video recordings' category: as will be explored further in the section on taxonomies, most users would have abandoned the search before reaching that point.

Some notations are unassigned in DDC; these provide gaps into which new subjects can be fitted. Of course, the success of this approach depends upon gaps being in the right places and it is very difficult to predict the areas in which new subjects are likely to arise. In taxonomy creation it is often assumed that new subjects can simply be fitted into the existing hierarchy. The problem with this ad hoc approach is that the structure becomes unbalanced and the taxonomy loses its efficiency as a finding tool.

'Other' classes are found throughout the DDC schedules: classes with non-specific titles to accommodate any subjects that may have been omitted when the scheme was first devised. Apart from being a useful device to accommodate unforeseen subjects, use of an 'Other' class is an inevitable consequence of Dewey's insistence on decimal structure: not every subject can be neatly divided into groups of ten. There is a potential problem with 'Miscellaneous' categories being used as a convenient dump for subjects that should have been accommodated elsewhere in a taxonomy.

Expressiveness is a desirable quality in an enumerative classification scheme. It refers to the ability of the notation to convey the hierarchical arrangement of subjects. This is useful in that readers can quickly identify narrower and broader topics. Also, as it is the notation that determines the shelf order of materials, an expressive notation will facilitate browsing: materials will be shelved in a way that makes explicit the relationships between topics in a subject area. But it is important to be consistent. It is not helpful if parts of the notation are expressive and other parts are not – users will be confused if the notation seems to indicate relationships that do not exist. An unfortunate fact is that expressiveness and hospitality are mutually exclusive. The display of hierarchy will break down as new subjects are added – it might very well not be possible to insert the new subject in a place where its notation will express its relationship to other topics. DDC's rigid structure should provide an ideal framework within which to develop expressive notation and generally DDC displays hierarchical relationships between subjects quite well and provides for a shelf arrangement that promotes browsing. However, expressiveness can suffer when new subjects are added and/or number building is applied. This is a problem that is not intrinsic to DDC; rather it is in the nature of hierarchies to start to break down as they grow in size and complexity, as we will see in our detailed examination of taxonomies later in the chapter.

A faceted classification scheme does not attempt to list subjects in the same exhaustive detail as an enumerative scheme. Instead it includes a listing of general concepts that can be combined, using notational synthesis, to represent compound subjects. In a faceted classification scheme it should be easy to accommodate new subjects: it is possible to extend faceted schemes because they are not rigidly structured like enumerative schemes – hospitality is increased because new subjects do not have to be inserted into an existing hierarchy. Expressiveness is not a feature normally associated with faceted classification schemes.

Universal Decimal Classification[18] has many features of a faceted classification scheme. It is, at first glance, very similar to Dewey from which it was developed, but there are important differences between the two schemes. In UDC various facet indicators are used to signify relationships between concepts. UDC allows two independently classifiable concepts to be linked; the nature of the relationship between the two subjects is indicated by the symbol used to link them.

There are three ways in which UDC achieves hospitality:

- decimal notation;
- gaps in the subject listing;
- faceted structure.

As described in the context of DDC, UDC allows for a new subject to be fitted almost anywhere in its sequence by using decimal subdivision and there are gaps in its listing of subjects into which new topics can be fitted. Additionally UDC's faceted structure often allows new subjects to be accommodated by linking previously unrelated topics. When interdisciplinary fields of study emerge, notations to represent them can be built using the existing schedules. This is a major advantage of using a faceted scheme for specialist collections – classifiers do not necessarily have to wait until revisions to the scheme are published to classify materials in emerging areas of knowledge.

Another example of a faceted scheme is Bliss Bibliographic Classification.[19] There are certain features of BC that ought to be briefly explained, because they are important to bear in mind in the context of taxonomies. First of all Bliss believed that an effective classification scheme should reflect the educational and scientific consensus; it should be based on the way in which specialists expect their knowledge to be organised: stressing the importance of user-centredness. Second, Bliss stressed the importance of collocation and subordination. Collocation means the bringing together of subjects that have a strong relationship to each other. Subordination means rather more than simply listing subjects from the general to the specific in this context. Bliss used subordination in the sense of gradation by speciality. This means that although a number of topics may be equally important, some can be seen as more specialised in that they draw on the findings of others. Subjects that are dependent in this way should follow the subjects on which they depend. The listing of the main classes in BC has been much admired, although subordination breaks down in the social sciences. For example, physics is based on mathematics and therefore must follow it in the list of main classes. Likewise, we use an understanding of physics in chemistry, and astronomy depends upon ideas generated in both physics and chemistry. This is an important concept in attempting to create a helpful order of subjects and display their relationships to one another, but very difficult to sustain in a linear expression of disciplines or subjects. A third important feature of BC is the provision of alternative locations. Bliss realised that no one order would satisfy everyone, so he provided two or more locations for certain subjects. For example, economic history could be included under general history or under economics: you choose the location which is most helpful to your library users. These are important features to bear in mind in taxonomy creation and the third feature will be discussed further.

Summary

All library classification schemes have schedules: the list of subjects. To summarise the features of library classification it is useful here to examine the criteria for an effective schedule, as the issues raised translate directly into taxonomy creation. Three areas are of particular concern:

- coverage;
- helpful order;
- provision for change.

Whether a scheme has been designed for use in general libraries or for a highly specialised collection of materials, it is essential that all topics of interest are included. Providing comprehensive coverage ought to include anticipating topics that are likely to emerge. This is, of course, a very difficult task, but in the library context emerging areas of knowledge are often covered in the journal and conference literature before being written up in book form. This emphasises the importance of subject expertise and keeping up to date with new developments in knowledge when devising a classification. In the organisational environment, needs analysis and content analysis will identify the subjects that must be represented in a taxonomy; strategic plans and policy documents may indicate emergent areas.

The schedules of a classification scheme should bring related subjects close together to establish a helpful order of materials on shelves. Shelf order should promote browsing, with the user being able to identify and scan both broad and narrow aspects of a topic. An expressive notation helps in this respect, with the user able to browse from the general to the specific and vice versa. Helpful order is not only important within subjects but also across subjects. Subjects that have some relationship to each other should be adjacent to each other in the schedules. For example, mathematics and physics are discrete and identifiable subject areas but have a relationship in that physics is based upon, and requires an understanding of, mathematics. Mathematics and physics should therefore be adjacent to each other in the schedules to demonstrate their relationship. New disciplines tend to be rather poorly represented in classification schemes that have a long history. Materials on subjects like women's studies and media studies are widely dispersed throughout the collection if a scheme like DDC is used. Newer disciplines tend not to restrict their sphere of interest within the traditional disciplines that were used to create main classes in DDC and other long established schemes. It is almost certainly the case that no classification scheme can establish a helpful order that meets the needs of all subjects and all users, but the schedules should reflect the widest possible consensus on how knowledge is structured. If a taxonomy is being created to organise a specialist collection of materials, then the order of subjects within it should take account of the expectations of the potential users of the collection.

Provision for change is absolutely essential. We have already considered the importance of hospitality, the ability to accommodate new subjects. As well being able to incorporate new subjects, it is also important that changing relationships between existing subjects can be expressed. New areas of knowledge tend to be increasingly interdisciplinary and any scheme should be able to accommodate emerging topics that span existing disciplines. Faceted schemes tend to be more hospitable than enumerative schemes. New topics can often be expressed by the combination of existing concepts in a faceted scheme, while enumerative schemes may require complete revision. Unfortunately, taxonomies tend to have more in common with enumerative classification than faceted. Taxonomies rely upon display of hierarchy: expressiveness is vitally important. Faceted schemes tend to lack expressiveness; they are hospitable because they are not expressive: new subjects can be added without compromising the structure of the scheme as a whole. As mentioned before, expressiveness and hospitality tend to be mutually exclusive: when hospitality is increased, expressiveness is sacrificed. As well as being able to accommodate new subjects, the schedules of classification schemes also have to reflect the current state of knowledge. Subjects have to be removed as well as added, and terminology used to name and describe subjects should reflect current usage. This means that regular revision is necessary.

Taxonomies

In the section on searching it was noted that most users will query a system using a single term or a simple phrase. As any information professional knows, it is easy to miss important information when conducting a keyword search: the relevance of the results is reliant on the quality of the indexing and the precision of the search statement as well as the availability of sophisticated search features like word stemming. Taxonomies provide a means of *finding* information, which it is helpful to differentiate from *searching* here. The ability to find information is dependent upon the information store being organised in a way that will promote browsing or foraging activities. A taxonomy organises information and knowledge in a meaningful way and, once the taxonomy has been constructed, users have access to a structured information store which is both searchable and browsable.

Introduction to taxonomy

The word 'taxonomy' has been with us for a very long time and it has most commonly been used in the context of classifying organisms – like the taxonomy of the animal kingdom presented in Chapter 1. That in fact illustrated very effectively what taxonomy in the context of information retrieval does. The most familiar type of taxonomy for information finding is exemplified in the subject tree arrangement of the web directories. A subject tree shows the relationships between subjects in a hierarchy which can be browsed: following links down the hierarchy to more specific subjects, or following links up the hierarchy to broader subjects. This is exactly the sort of structure traditional classification schemes like Dewey impose on knowledge. This is exactly the sort of structure web directories like the Open Directory impose on web resources (see Figure 3.9).

At the top of the Open Directory's hierarchy are 16 subjects – the equivalent of main classes in a library classification scheme. If we want to

Figure 3.9 Open Directory: home page

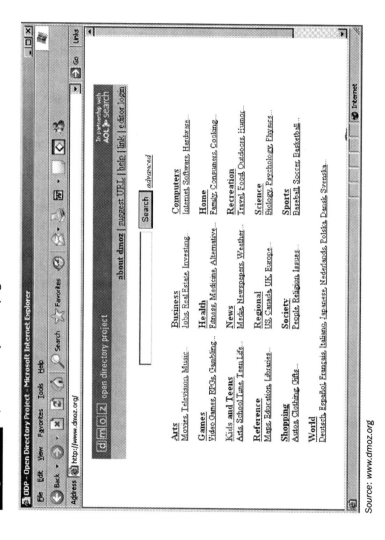

find out which web resources on Information Architecture the Open Directory indexes we first have to decide which of these categories might include our topic. The simplest route is to follow the link to Reference (see Figure 3.10) – that is the simplest route, but not necessarily the obvious one.

Next we click on Knowledge Management. Here we see a link to Information Architecture (see Figure 3.11).

If we click on that link we find four more categories and some suggestions about other parts of the hierarchy we might find relevant information in, plus a list of individual sites and web resources (see Figure 3.12).

In using a taxonomy or subject tree we basically continue following links until we reach a level of the hierarchy that contains the specific information we need or we give up because it is taking us too long to find anything useful.

So what the Open Directory is doing is essentially what library classification schemes do. It has main classes and sub-classes. It brings related subjects together and keeps them apart from unrelated subjects. The structure, as in traditional classification schemes, is hierarchical: expressive. If we are just dealing with classification, why is there so much interest in taxonomies? The argument is that:

> Taxonomies provide a means for designing vastly enhanced searching, browsing and filtering systems. They can be used to relieve the user from the burden of sifting specific information from the large and low-quality response of most popular search engines. Querying with respect to a taxonomy is more reliable than depending on presence or absence of specific keywords.[20]

A well structured taxonomy can increase the efficiency of retrieval and decrease user effort. Quality control is exercised by the human indexer who will assign documents to categories. Users of the resource do not have to construct and modify a search statement, and they do not have to scan several pages of results in an attempt to find the information they need.

There are, however, four problems associated with taxonomies or subject trees which will now be explored in some detail.

- lack of vocabulary control;
- ad hoc addition of new subject categories;
- limitations of hierarchies;
- limitations of human indexing.

Figure 3.10 Open Directory: Reference category

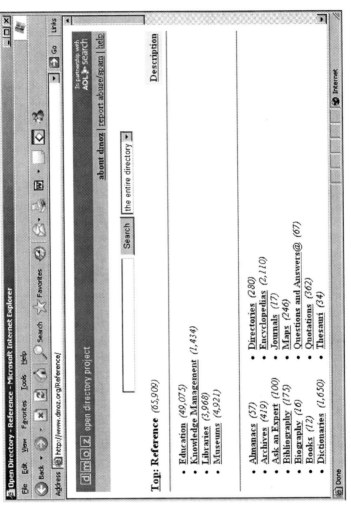

Source: http//www.dmoz.org/Reference/

Figure 3.11 Open Directory: Knowledge Management category

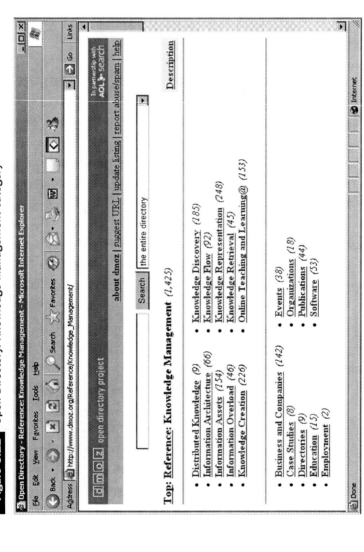

Source: http//www.dmoz.org/Reference/Knowledge_Management/

Figure 3.12 Open Directory: Information Architecture category

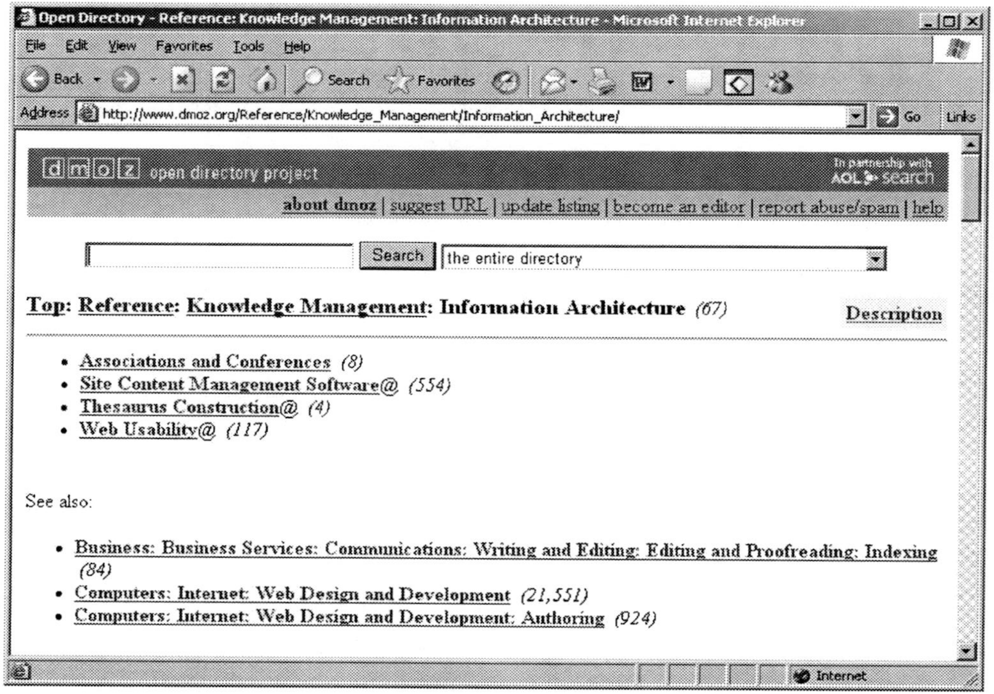

Source: http://www.dmoz.org/Reference/Knowledge_Management/Information_Architecture/

Web directories are pre-coordinate indexes; coordination of terms is performed by the indexer when they assign a document to a category or categories. Something that is generally agreed to be essential in pre-coordinate indexes is vocabulary control. Although the naming and listing of subject categories in web directories like those provided by Open Directory and Yahoo can be said to impose some sort of vocabulary control, the problem is that there is a lack of consistency in use of terms even within the subject tree provided by a single web directory. This lack of consistency in use of terms is even more apparent if the subject trees of several web directories are compared. To compound the problem there is not only inconsistent naming of categories there is also inconsistent placing of categories within the hierarchy – in traditional classification schemes there is at least pretty general agreement of how knowledge is structured.

Librarians using traditional classification schemes like Dewey Decimal often have problems when new subjects emerge because it takes a while for the scheme to be revised to accommodate them. Web directory indexers do not have that problem: they can simply create a new category and find a place for it within the existing subject tree. If you monitor some web directories (particularly those aimed at a popular market) you will find that they seem to change even their top level categories (main classes) on a regular and completely ad hoc basis.

Hierarchies are generally quite effective ways to map subjects, but as is apparent when looking at any traditional hierarchical classification scheme, hierarchies tend to break down as their size and complexity increases. In library classification schemes expressiveness suffers as developments in knowledge are added – it is an unfortunate consequence of being hospitable to new subjects.

In considering the limitations of human indexing, it is possible to identify three major issues: the size of the index, the currency of the index and consistency. Human indexers obviously work more slowly than a software package automatically indexing web resources. Consequently the indexes of web directories are a lot smaller than those of the search engines. At the time of writing, Google claimed to index more than eight billion URLs,[21] while the Open Directory (the largest of the web directories) could only claim to index four million sites.[22] Four million sites would include many more individual URLs, which in a direct comparison with Google's claim would increase the Open Directory's coverage, but it is still a fraction of that of the major search engines. Providers of web directories would argue that they provide greater quality control, that only authoritative sites are included in their listings, but nonetheless size matters.

Often when using a web directory you will find yourself following the hierarchy to sites or pages that no longer exist. As noted previously, human indexers work more slowly than automatic indexing systems, and keeping the hierarchy current is a huge problem. Information on the Web is often so transient that no retrieval system can claim to be right up to date. It is more difficult for web directories where documents are added and links are created by human indexers to be up to date. We will return to this issue in Chapter 6 on management and maintenance.

In terms of consistency, human indexers have to decide how to categorise a website or page: does it fit into an existing category? if so, which category does it fit into? if there does not seem to be an appropriate category, then is it necessary to create a new one? This takes us back to the problem of ad hoc addition of categories. The teams of people working on indexing the web for directories like the Open Directory (which relies on volunteers) and Yahoo do not have a lot of time for subject analysis and they can classify items wrongly: which means they end up in the wrong category in the wrong part of the hierarchy. In one sense it is easier for librarians working with schemes like Dewey Decimal because they are so much more sophisticated and detailed than the subject tree hierarchies used on the web; you are more likely to find a place in the hierarchy for the document you are classifying. In another sense it is much more difficult for librarians because a book can only be shelved in one place – at least web indexers can categorise an item in more than one place in the subject tree.

Unfortunately there is no solution to some of these problems. Hierarchies have inherent limitations and we have to live with them. What would help to maintain consistency would be some sort of standardisation: a formal classification scheme for web resources that would provide a standardised subject tree structure and would also ensure vocabulary control. The Open Directory is the closest thing we have to a standard but there is a lack of cooperation between the providers of web directories. Various projects are exploring the possibility of replacing the human indexer with software to achieve automatic classification of resources: at OCLC the possibility of using Dewey Decimal for automatic classification of the web has been explored. But, at the moment, there is no real alternative to the human classifier, so consistency will remain a problem even though standardisation would of course help by imposing a formal hierarchy within which items would be classified or categorised. An argument against standardisation is that it would reduce choice, and that is a valid argument in the context of the web: users can choose the type of subject tree that meets their needs – one that specialises in ring tones or one that specialises in conference papers. In the context of an organisation's taxonomy, standardisation should be enforced through vocabulary control and use of metadata. These issues will be explored in the next chapter.

Monohierarchies and polyhierarchies

The above section has dealt with the subject tree approach to taxonomy building, which is based upon the principles of enumerative classification schemes with expressiveness being the central concept. In this type of monohierarchy, the basic rule is that categories should be both exhaustive and mutually exclusive. This means that there must be an appropriate category for each subject, and only one category for each, with no subject appearing more than once in the hierarchy or subject tree. As the taxonomy grows this is increasingly difficult to sustain, and in practice you will find that individual categories do appear in several places within the subject tree. Duplication of categories is a contentious issue and some organisations have adopted multiple hierarchies in an attempt to solve the problem of duplication and to accommodate specialist needs. This means that there may be several taxonomies: an overarching taxonomy for general use, plus a series of taxonomies for specialist user groups.

Another approach, based on principles of faceted classification, is to embrace duplication of categories and develop polyhierarchies. Here duplication of categories is not seen as a problem but rather as essential to express relationships between subjects and to meet the needs of users. Given the tendency of hierarchies to break down as more subjects are added, this is a very sensible approach. There has been a resurgence of interest in faceted classification, as its principles are applied to web organisation and retrieval (see also the section on ontologies in the next chapter). The subject listing in a faceted classification scheme is much shorter than in an enumerative scheme because the faceted scheme includes only basic concepts plus rules for how those concepts can be synthesised to represent compound subjects. Faceted schemes recognise that a single concept can be attached to many other concepts represented in the subject listing: fewer subjects are listed, but overall coverage is extensive because of the flexible way in which individual subjects can be combined. This is impossible to reproduce in a monohierarchy, where concepts can only be listed once. Thesauri, which are examined in depth in the next chapter, also work on the principle that subjects are not mutually exclusive. Thesauri map hierarchical relationships between subjects: identifying broader and narrower concepts. So, for example, the basic concept of 'dogs' would be a narrower term for both domestic animals and working animals: this means that a 'dog' category should appear under both of those concepts in a taxonomy. Web directories actually make quite extensive use of polyhierarchies. For example, in the Open Directory there are several routes to the Library and Information Science category:

Reference > Libraries > Library and Information Science
Society > Social Sciences > Library and Information Science
Science > Social Sciences > Library and Information Science

This is essentially the same device as Bliss used in his Bibliographic Classification: provision of alternative locations, and is very easy to implement in the digital environment. The content of the Library and Information Science category is the same whatever route is taken to reach it; the taxonomy creator has simply linked the category to several others at higher levels in the hierarchy. Boiko says that: 'In a faceted classification, the idea of polyhierarchy is taken to the extreme. Items are listed in as many categories as possible, but the number of levels in the overall hierarchy ... is kept to a minimum.'[23] This highlights another advantage of the polyhierarchical approach: the taxonomy will be typically broader and shallower than the monohierarchical approach, and this is much more efficient for users who will tend to abandon their search after three or four mouse clicks.

There is a potential disadvantage associated with polyhierarchies: disorientation. Suppose we follow links to the Information Architecture category in the Open Directory (Figure 3.13). Perhaps we want information about Web Usability so we click on that category (Figure 3.14). Here we have a lot of company information plus some more categories, plus a long list of individual web resources and sites. At this point we might become disoriented, because we suddenly find ourselves in a different part of the subject tree – as you can see from the breadcrumbs at the top of the screen. This is not terribly helpful, and we have done a lot of drilling down the hierarchy without necessarily finding documentation we need. A better approach might have been to have used a 'see also' link rather than duplicating the category name as a link under information architecture.

Figure 3.13 Polyhierarchies – Open Directory: Information Architecture category

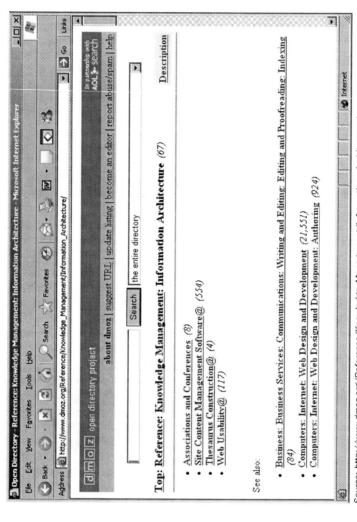

Figure 3.14 Open Directory: Web Usability

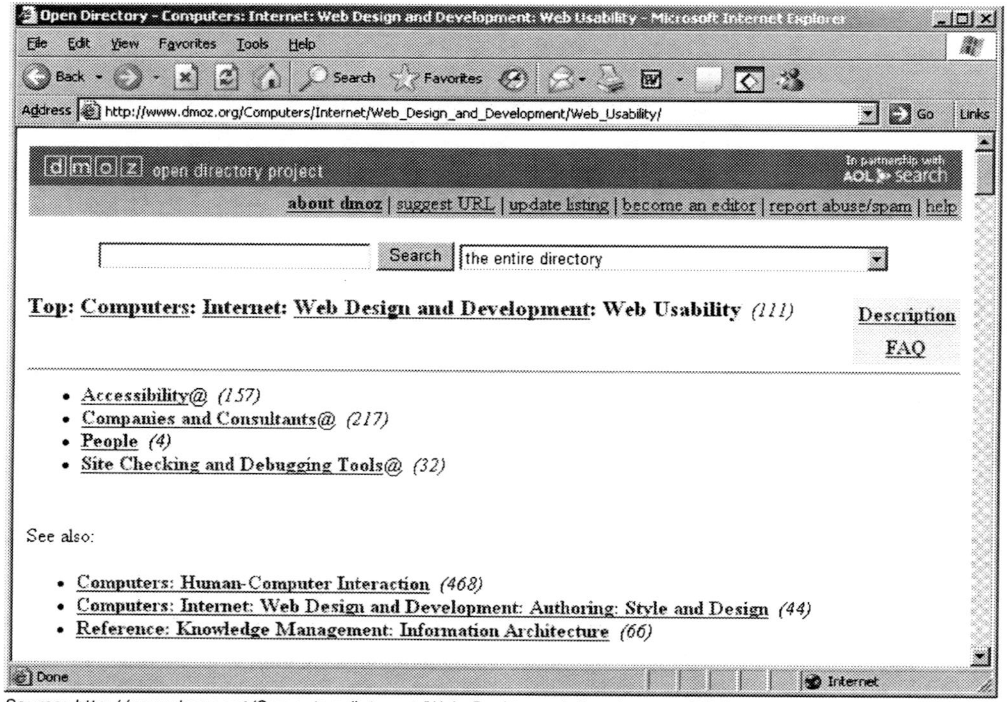

Source: http://www.dmoz.org/Computers/Internet/Web_Design_and_Development/Web_Usability/

Taxonomy building

The preliminaries

It is important, first, to remind you that any development impacting upon an organisation's information and knowledge resources must be informed by a thorough analysis of organisational needs, individual user needs, tasks and individual resources as examined in detail in Chapter 2. The next stage would be a more specific subject analysis of electronic information and knowledge resources. Successful subject analysis relies upon an understanding of the content, the value and the use of information and knowledge resources, based upon an understanding of the needs and characteristics of the users of those resources. So the subject analysis should follow the needs analysis. We examine subject analysis and content analysis in the next chapter, where the focus is on documents.

Structure

How an organisation structures its taxonomy is obviously dependent upon the outcomes of the information audit and the subject analysis, but it is possible to state some general principles. The basic structure of the taxonomy will be: main classes, the categories at the top level of the hierarchy, leading to a series of sub-classes, lower-level categories, down to document level. It is good practice to limit the number of top-level categories; users do not want to be overwhelmed with choice at the start of their browsing activities. The second level (immediately below the top level) can contain a greater number of categories. It is recommended that the depth of the hierarchy should not exceed five levels; users will become frustrated and will abandon their search if the hierarchy is too deep.

We have seen in the previous section that it is not always possible, or desirable, to adhere to the 'no duplication of category names' rule. Individual organisations will have to decide whether they develop a single monohierarchy, multiple hierarchies or a polyhierarchy. The point of the taxonomy is that it should be simple to use and that it should help people to find the information they need. This means, in general, taking whichever approach results in a broad and shallow hierarchy. Polyhierarchies are the most common. Critics may say that the reason for this is that they are easier to construct: less care needs to be taken in creating the hierarchy if categories can be duplicated. Supporters of the approach would say that polyhierarchies offer more effective browsing environments because they cater for a variety of approaches and reflect the inherent ambiguity of information items, as well as allowing for shallower hierarchies.

Care must be taken in naming the categories or subjects. Any ambiguous terms should certainly be avoided. It helps if individuals within the organisation have a shared understanding of terminology: that shared understanding should not, of course, be assumed. Consistency is important – you should use or create an index or thesaurus to provide a form of vocabulary control: this will help when documents are being indexed and added to the system and will also help in creating the subject categories themselves. Using a very simplistic example from web directories, some have the category 'computing', others have 'computers'. Avoid this type of inconsistency: you should decide which word form is going to be used and then use it consistently. Concepts of vocabulary control are explored further in the next chapter.

Creating the hierarchy is a very difficult and complex task. Subjects should be at a level in the hierarchy that reflects their relationship with other subjects: for example, how broad or how narrow they are. As has been noted, a hierarchical structure tends to break down as more subjects are added. Expressiveness suffers, with some subjects appearing much lower down in their part of the hierarchy than their status merits, and others appearing much higher up. It is actually very difficult to consistently portray a subject's status by its level within the hierarchy. In both monohierarchies and polyhierarchies this seems to be an insoluble problem: it is an inherent property of hierarchies, so there is not much you can do about it, but you must be aware of it and try to maintain consistency of subdivision as best you can.

There are, traditionally, two approaches to building a hierarchy: the top-down and the bottom-up. There is often a temptation to begin by naming the top-level categories and then start working down through the various levels until the most specific subject descriptors are reached. This may be too restrictive: when individual documents are analysed you may find that they do not seem to fit into the top-level categories you have devised. The temptation then is to create more top-level categories. A better approach may be to start with the specific and then work up to the general. A problem with the bottom-up approach is that you may be overwhelmed with the detail and find it difficult to identify patterns. As well as the top-down and the bottom-up, a third approach has been suggested: the middle-out.[24] Here it is suggested that the process should begin with a definition of the most fundamental or basic terms before seeking more general and more specific terms. So, for example, classification would be identified as a basic term and that could lead to broader terms such as indexing and narrower terms such as Dewey Decimal Classification and Library of Congress Classification.

Having established the basic structure, categories within levels have to be organised in some way. Library classification schemes adopt a logical approach to ordering concepts: for example, regional medicine in Dewey Decimal has a top-down order, starting with the head and moving down to the lower extremities. If a commonly understood logic can be identified, then it is useful to apply it in the listing of category names. Another approach is a sequential listing: if a category consists of links to a number of processes that should be performed sequentially, then they can be presented in the order in which they should be performed. The easiest, and most commonly understood, ordering is a simple alphabetical arrangement. This is the approach taken by web directories and is certainly most appropriate when scanning long lists of names. At the bottom of the hierarchy will be links to individual documents and they should also be organised in some way: alphabetically by author or title, chronologically, with the most recent first, for example.

Maintenance of the taxonomy

Various issues are involved in maintaining the taxonomy post-creation. It is useful to consider the following maintenance issues at this point:

- adding new categories;
- adding documents;
- removing documents.

The creation of new categories should not be done on an ad hoc basis. Vocabulary control is important here to help maintain consistency of naming when creating new categories, but you should first ask: is a new category needed or can this document be accommodated within an existing category or categories? If care was taken in creating the taxonomy in the first place, then it should have been possible to anticipate some developments and to have created categories accordingly. When new categories are added to the taxonomy will the hierarchy start to break down? You might find that one part of your hierarchy is expanding enormously while other parts remain relatively stable. Is it appropriate to expand vertically or should you expand horizontally? Think about consistency of subdivision and ensuring that a category's level within the hierarchy reflects its relationship with others.

In terms of adding documents we are moving beneath the surface level and looking at the electronic resources themselves. Precise classification of documents is not as crucial in the electronic environment as it is in the traditional library environment. A single document can be linked to several different categories to allow for individual needs and expertise. At the same time, it is not good practice to overload the system with links because that will affect its use. It is important to avoid inclusion of inappropriate or redundant links: it will just take people longer to find what they need if they are bombarded with irrelevant information when they explore a category.

So far the focus has been on adding resources to the taxonomy – what about 'weeding'? It has already been suggested that the taxonomy loses its efficiency as more and more categories and resources are added to it. Is it therefore necessary to remove dated documents or those that are no longer relevant? Essentially, maintaining a taxonomy is like maintaining any library: materials have to be removed as well as added.

Summary

One thing which should be apparent is that building and maintaining a taxonomy is a very complex task, and a great deal of thought has to go into the process. Knowledge management companies offer taxonomy packages and consultancy, and organisations of all kinds are getting involved in the process of building and maintaining their taxonomies. However, in their enthusiasm to embrace taxonomies, organisations have not necessarily grasped the complexity of what they are getting involved in, and the general picture seems to be quite chaotic. The situation is not helped by the lack of agreement about what a taxonomy actually is: organisations are creating their own definitions and building their taxonomies on the basis of what they think they need, or they are building their taxonomies on the basis of what a commercial package can provide. The result is that there are a lot of poorly designed taxonomies that do not provide a structured finding tool and do not add any value to an information system.

Overview

In this chapter the focus has been upon information retrieval through searching and finding. A recurring concept throughout this book is that of user-centredness, and we have seen that in order to accommodate individual information seeking strategies, a range of search and browsing tools should be provided. The ability of users to find information through exploring categories in a taxonomy and the ability of the system to search for and retrieve information in response to user queries is dependent upon how documents are stored, tagged and organised. This leads into elements of document analysis and description which are explored in the next chapter.

Further reading

An excellent introduction to the complexity of search behaviour and the development of search strategies is found in:

- Bates, M.J. (1989) 'The design of browsing and berrypicking techniques for the online search interface', *Online Review*, 13 (5): 407–24.

Anyone requiring a more in-depth treatment will find Kuhlthau's book useful:

- Kuhlthau, C.C. (1993) *Seeking Meaning: A Process Approach to Library and Information Systems*. Norwood, NJ: Ablex.

For a simple introduction to concepts of information search and retrieval the following is recommended:

- Large, A. et al. (1999) *Information Seeking in the Online Age: Principles and Practice*. London: Bowker Saur.

Anyone wishing to explore concepts further should look at:

- Chowdhury, G.C. (2004) *Introduction to Modern Information Retrieval*, 2nd edn. London: Facet.

Also recommended is:

- Marchionini, G. (1997) *Information Seeking in Electronic Environments*. Cambridge: Cambridge University Press.

Two sites are recommended for anyone wishing to find out more about search engines and their search features:

- *http://www.searchengineshowdown.com* – the site includes reviews and links to the various search engines covered. It is worth exploring some of the lesser known search engines.

- *http://www.searchenginewatch.com* – the site includes search engine listings and search tips as well as other useful information.

For a practical introduction to classification and taxonomy:

- Batley, S. (2005) *Classification in Theory and Practice.* Oxford: Chandos.

For a more in-depth exploration of classification theories:

- Broughton, V. (2004) *Essential Classification.* London: Facet.

References

1. Kuhlthau, C.C. (1993) *Seeking Meaning: A Process Approach to Library and Information Systems.* Norwood, NJ: Ablex.
2. Bates, M.J. (1989) 'The design of browsing and berrypicking techniques for the online search interface', *Online Review*, 13 (5): 407–24.
3. Large, A. et al. (1999) *Information Seeking in the Online Age: Principles and Practice.* London: Bowker Saur, p. 179.
4. Harter, S.P. (1986) *Online Information Retrieval: Concepts, Principles and Techniques.* Orlando, FL: Academic Press.
5. Ibid.
6. Salton, G. (ed.) (1971) *The SMART Retrieval System: Experiments in Automatic Document Processing.* Upper Saddle River, NJ: Prentice-Hall.
7. Hildreth, C. (1982) 'The concept and mechanics of browsing in an online library catalogue', in *Proceedings of the Third National Online Meeting.* London: Learned Information.
8. Palay, A.J. and Fox, M.S. (1981) 'Browsing through databases', in R.N. Oddy et al. (eds), *Information Retrieval Research.* London: Butterworth.
9. Hildreth, op, cit., p. 181.
10. Meadow, C.T. (1970) *Man–Machine Communication.* London: Wiley, p. 124.
11. Search for 'hazardous substances': *http://www.google.co.uk* (accessed 8 August 2006).
12. Alta Vista special search terms: *http://www.altavista.com/help/ search/syntax* (accessed 14 August 2006).

13. Exalead help pages: *http://www.exalead.com/search/C=0/?2p=Help .1* (accessed 15 August 2006).
14. Northern Light: *http://www.northernlight.com/* (accessed 15 August 2006).
15. Search Engine Showdown, Features Chart: *http://www .searchengineshowdown.com/features/* (accessed 16 August 2006).
16. Library of Congress Classification: *http://www.loc.gov/catdir/cpso/ lcco/lcco.html* (accessed 16 August 2006).
17. Dewey Decimal Classification: *http://www.oclc.org/dewey/* (accessed 16 August 2006).
18. Universal Decimal Classification: *http://www.udcc.org/* (accessed 16 August 2006).
19. Bliss Classification Association: *http://www.sid.cam.ac.uk/bca/ bcahome.htm* (accessed 16 August 2006).
20. Chakrabarti, S. et al. (1998) 'Scalable feature selection, classification and signature generation for organizing large text databases into hierarchical topic taxonomies', *VLDB Journal*, 7: 163–78.
21. Google Inc. fact sheet: *http://www.google.co.uk/press/facts.html* (accessed 17 August 2006).
22. Open Directory: *http://www.dmoz.org* (accessed 17 August 2006).
23. Boiko, B. (2005) *Content Management Bible*, 2nd edn. Indianapolis, IN: Wiley, p. 659.
24. Uschold, M. and Gruninger, M. (1996) 'Ontologies: principles, methods and applications', *Knowledge Engineering Review*, 11 (2): 93–155.

Documents and document description

As explored in Chapter 1 definitions of information vary somewhat, but most will concentrate on information being more than data and less than knowledge. Information is data that has been organised in some way: in the text of a book, journal article or report, in a video, in a multimedia presentation. Knowledge is information that has been assimilated and put to use on a personal level: understanding of a subject or a process, an increased awareness of how to make use of information. This three part model: data > information > knowledge, is widely understood and used in explaining concepts of information and knowledge management. Here it is useful to introduce a fourth element: data > information > content > knowledge. Boiko cites a definition of content: 'Raw information becomes content when it is given a usable form intended for one or more purposes.'[1] Content is information and data combined: a document contains information, and when that document has been described, organised and given metadata tags it becomes content. Information systems provide access to content, information architecture structures that content. Content is a central concern: its analysis, description and retrieval – through searching and finding or browsing. In the previous chapter we looked at searching and finding strategies and tools; in this chapter the focus is on the information itself (documents) and on adding value: transforming information into content.

This chapter is divided into two main sections:

- *Document description and content analysis*: analysing the whole range of an organisation's subject content, and analysing the content of individual documents. The organisational content analysis will feed into the overall structure of the information system, particularly the taxonomy. Individual document analysis will result in the assigning of metadata tags that will assist in adding content to the taxonomy and assist its retrieval through a search engine.

- *Thesaurus creation and ontologies*: examining the concepts of vocabulary control and the identification of semantic relationships as means of adding value to information retrieval systems. Again our concern is with making search and retrieval more efficient.

Document description and content analysis

There is often a temptation to think about information architecture in terms of the surface architecture, concentrating on how information is presented and how users interact with the information system. But at the heart of the system is its content: information architecture provides effective access to an organisation's information content. As an essential step in understanding how to search for and retrieve information we need to move below the surface or the system interface to examine the information itself – looking at elements of bibliographic or document description and content analysis. This is obviously vitally important. No matter how well designed the system, it is only going to be of benefit if it includes all the documentation and information its users need, and if that information and documentation can be easily retrieved and utilised.

So far in this book we have examined high-level content by considering, first, user needs: what problems face people within the organisation and what information they need access to in order to resolve those problems; and, second, the representation of subjects in a taxonomy: categorising subjects and placing them within a browsable hierarchy. This is a top-down approach to system content, representing an ideal. At this point we need to consider what actually exists in the system and the type of documentation that is created within the organisation – how to review and manage individual information items. The reality will not necessarily match the vision.

This brings us into the field of records management, so a good place to begin is to define the term 'record'. The Association of Records Managers and Administrators (ARMA) defines a record as: 'Recorded information, regardless of medium or characteristics, made or retrieved by an organisation that is useful in the operation of the organisation.'[2] This is obviously a very broad definition, but the implication that the form or medium of the record is secondary to the information it carries is important. This is emphasised on the ARMA website:

> It's estimated that more than 90% of the records being created today are electronic. Coupled with the overwhelming growth of electronic messages – most notably e-mail and instant messaging – the management of electronic records has become a critical business issue. How that information is managed has significant business, legal, and technology ramifications. Ultimately, it doesn't matter what medium is used to create, deliver, or store information when determining if content is a record and should be managed accordingly.[3]

The clear implication here is that records management is selective. A lot of documentation, a lot of content, will be produced and acquired by an organisation, but not everything will merit the status of a record. It is only the records that need to be stored and made accessible to system users.

Schwartz and Hernon[4] emphasise the same point but take it a stage further when they say that records can be characterised by form, status and function. They also make the point that form is an important consideration in storage and retrieval, but that it is the record's status and function that determine its value. Status refers to the activity and permanency of the record, function refers to the role it plays within the organisation. In terms of status some records will be of transient interest while others will need to be accessible for longer periods. In terms of function some records will be of general interest and importance and will need to be widely available while others may be of interest only to limited numbers of specialist users within the organisation.

So we need to determine what merits definition as a record: documentation that needs to be made accessible on an information system, and we need to determine the status and function of such a record. This brings us into the field of content analysis. It was noted earlier that so far in this book we have looked at high-level content, a top-down approach, in our examination of information needs and taxonomy creation. Now we need to change our focus. Rosenfeld and Morville say that:

> Content analysis is a defining component of the bottom-up approach to architecture, involving careful review of the documents and objects that actually exist. What's in the site may

not match the visions articulated by the strategy team and the opinion leaders. You'll need to identify and address these gaps between top-down vision and bottom-up reality.[5]

A lot of documentation will exist within an organisation and within its information systems and services. A lot of that documentation might not possess the status and function that will define it as a record. Part of developing the information architecture will involve examining the documentation, deciding what should and should not be present in the system, and drawing up guidelines for authoring and content management. Content management is something that we will be returning to in Chapter 6 on management and maintenance; here the focus will be on content gathering, analysis and mapping.

There is no quick and easy way to analyse content. No existing formula or software package is going to take into account the needs of a particular organisation. For the information architect as content analyst there are no real short cuts, but the process can be helped by adhering to some practical guidelines. A sensible first step is to try to identify and gather a representative sample of documents. Rosenfeld and Morville[6] suggest a 'Noah's Ark' approach to content gathering: try to capture a couple of each type of animal. They divide species of document according to the following:

- *Format.* Any organisation will have documents in a variety of different paper and digital formats: paper and electronic text, audio-visual materials and software applications, for example.

- *Document type.* Documentation will be produced for a range of purposes from current awareness and marketing to training and research and development. Examples of document types would include news articles, technical reports, presentations, brochures and so on. Boiko supplies a comprehensive list of core content or document types[7] that could be used as metadata tags.

- *Source.* We examined organisational structure in Chapter 2. As part of the process of content analysis you will need to get representative documents from all the different departments within the organisation: customer support, marketing, research and development, human resources and so on.

- *Subject.* Obviously, representative documents would have to represent the whole range of the organisation's subject interests. To assist here you can use categories already established in the organisation's taxonomy, or you can use its thesaurus or classification scheme if any of these tools already exist.

- *Existing architecture.* Assuming some kind of information system is already in place, you can take a sample of the documentation that already exists within the system.

When the representative documentation has been gathered, the content analysis can begin. We will be looking again at a detailed breakdown of content later in the chapter when we look at metadata. At this point it is helpful to take a more general approach by concentrating on content mapping and subject description. When you are analysing individual documents there are four questions to keep in mind:

- What is this?
- How can this be described?
- What distinguishes this from other documents?
- How can this document be made retrievable?

Obviously, the 'What is this?' question is the most general, and can be answered by looking at format, document type, source and subject. We have already seen that the format should not actually matter, as long as software is available to access the content, although some formats like paper and video may need to be transferred to other media to be mounted on the system, or may need to be stored separately. Who created the document and the type of document (annual report, technical report and so on) are also not really terribly important. It is the information content of the document that determines its status and function as a record, so that is where the focus of the analysis should lie. The information content is also addressed in the other three questions: 'How can this be described?', 'What distinguishes this from other documents?' and 'How can this document be made retrievable?' We will look at subject analysis and selection of index terms later. First it is useful to look at content mapping, which partly addresses these three questions and will help in determining status and function.

Content mapping is focused on what Boiko calls 'content components' within documents.[8] Alternative names include 'information chunks', 'content objects' and 'reusable information objects', among others. Rosenfeld and Morville prefer the term 'information chunk' which they define as: 'the most finely grained portion of content that merits or requires individual treatment'.[9] Content mapping seeks to find answers to more questions:

- Can this document be segmented into multiple chunks that users might want to access separately?

- What is the smallest section of document content that needs to be individually indexed?
- Will the content of this document need to be repurposed across multiple documents or as part of multiple processes?[10]

Finding answers to these questions involves identifying content components or information chunks. First of all, can content components be identified? Secondly, how small are the components? Thirdly, will individual components be reused across different documents or for different purposes? This last question obviously addresses the function or role of the content – in fact, a content component is essentially a record. Each component will have a status and a function (and a form) that will merit its definition as a discrete record. So, it is not the document itself that is a record, rather it is the individual components of information content within it that are the records that need to be managed.

Figure 4.1 provides a personal narrative that illustrates how a single document contains several records that can be reused across different applications for different audiences.

All information systems contain a lot of records or content components that are reused in different documents. Identifying and mapping the individual records or components is time-consuming initially, but will ultimately save time and effort. It will help to avoid duplication – creating and storing the same information several times – and will allow updating of information on the system to be achieved quickly and efficiently.

To make all this economy possible, the information architecture has to identify relationships between the chunks or records. Rosenfeld and Morville identify four different types of relationship that can exist between content components:[11]

- *Sequencing*. Chunks can be placed together in a sequence. Processes are very often sequential, for example a job description followed by information on how to apply.
- *Co-location*. Even though the information they contain stands alone, value is added when the chunks are placed in the same document. Job descriptions and information about how to apply should be located on the same page.
- *Linking*. Chunks can link to other chunks. Hypertext links can be inserted to link to other chunks or records within other documents. Job details can link to information about the organisation.
- *Shared meaning*. Even if chunks are not explicitly linked, they can share semantic characteristics that ensure they are co-located in an

Figure 4.1	Content components: one document, many uses

Courses at London Metropolitan University are comprised of various modules dealing with specific aspects of a subject. For every module taught in the university detailed documentation is produced in the form of a module specification, which includes a comprehensive description of the module and details of the course or courses it is part of. The original specification that is written when a new module is being developed can be broken down into content components or chunks: adherence to university and postgraduate school regulations, aims and learning outcomes, syllabus, assessment instruments, suggested readings, and so on. All of those chunks ought to be individually retrievable and all should be reusable.

The original documentation is prepared when the module is validated by the university, but chunks are reused in lots of different contexts. Some of the content of my module specifications goes on 'postgradline', the part of the University website where current and prospective students can find out about courses and modules; some of the content goes into the students' module booklets; some of the content goes into documentation for CILIP accreditation; reading lists will be made accessible via the library web pages, and so on. If the content chunks have been defined and identified, and mapped onto the information architecture as records in their own right, records that have a status and function, then if I want to update reading lists, for example, I would not have to change every piece of documentation; changing the content of the chunk containing the reading list would update all the documents that contain that content.

ad hoc manner. A search engine would find details of other jobs with the same title or in the same department.

The personal narrative continues in Figure 4.2 to illustrate the four types of relationship.

Document or content analysis is essential in managing the content of the information system. Prior to system implementation existing documentation should be analysed, document types identified, records or content components identified and the records mapped onto each other so that they can be reused across multiple documents. Once the initial analysis has been completed, there should be considerable savings in time, effort and efficiency. Templates for document creation can be used to promote consistency and to ensure that records are identified and tagged at the authoring stage. Once a record has been created it can be incorporated into many documents for many purposes, reducing duplication of effort and the amount of storage capacity needed. Documents can be updated quickly

Figure 4.2   Relationships

- *Sequencing.* In my module specification, the week-by-week guide to the module content should start at week 1 and continue sequentially through to week 11. Each week's content stands alone as a record or chunk, but can also be presented as a sequence. A temporal sequence can be identified for assessment instruments, with one piece of coursework being due for submission earlier in the module than another. It is often possible to identify a sequential relationship between content components.

- *Co-location.* All the content components are co-located within the original module specification. Other, smaller clusters can also be identified: for example, assessment instruments have to be mapped onto the module aims and learning outcomes, so it is sensible to have all of those chunks on the same web page.

- *Linking.* In my module specification, there can be a link from my name as module convenor to the information about me on the Information Management staff pages. The content of the reading list can link to the library website for information about whether there are loan copies of books available.

- *Shared meaning.* If I create metadata for my module specification and include subject tags, or if the text of the module specification is automatically indexed, then anyone searching under the metadata tag or typing in a subject name or phrase in a search engine will retrieve my module specification, plus all the other records that include the same metadata or the same text.

because changing a single record will mean that all documentation containing that record will include the changes.

Content is at the heart of the information architecture and we return to it when content management is explored in Chapter 6. But before content can be managed it has to be identified, analysed and organised. So far in this chapter we have examined general aspects of content analysis. Now we move on to a more specific issue: that of document description and metadata creation.

Metadata

The term metadata has been around since at least the 1960s, but it is only with the development of the web that literature on the subject has proliferated. In the past few years there has been an enormous amount of information management literature generated on this topic as the information profession has realised that what the computer scientists have been writing about is something we already know a great deal about: cataloguing. The term metadata simply translates to 'data about data' which is not particularly helpful in explaining its purpose or value. A rather more detailed definition is provided by Vellucci: 'data that describe attributes of a resource, characterise its relationships, support its discovery and effective use, and exist in an electronic environment'.[12] This should sound very familiar to any information professional because a catalogue record is metadata about, for example, a library book. Although metadata has come to be associated almost exclusively with electronic information as stated in Vellucci's definition, traditional library catalogues contain metadata for information published in any format – books, manuscripts, maps, videos and so on.

Haynes[13] says that metadata has five purposes:

- resource description;
- information retrieval;
- management of information;
- rights management, ownership and authenticity;
- interoperability and e-commerce;

Resource description underpins the other four functions of metadata. At this level the focus is essentially upon cataloguing. In the digital, as in the traditional library environment, adequate description of resources means that the associated metadata can be used for retrieval, records management and so on. Every resource has identifiable elements that can be used to describe it and differentiate it from other resources. These would include its title, the date it was produced, its creator and its format, for example. Consistent and detailed resource description hugely increases the efficiency of systems for the retrieval and management of information.

Efficiency of retrieval is a fundamental concern. We have all used search engines to retrieve information from the web. We have all, at some point, been frustrated because the results of our searches have included a lot of non-relevant information. That is always a potential problem with automatic indexing and it is a problem which is magnified in web searching, first because of the sheer size of the index being searched, and second because of the way its documents are structured (or not structured). This can be contrasted with searching for information using a legacy host like Dialog. It is important to note that many of the Dialog databases contain records about journal articles, not the articles themselves; in fact many Dialog records contain metadata about the original journal articles. When using Dialog, once we have mastered the commands, searches almost certainly tend to produce fewer non-relevant items than when using a search engine on the web. One obvious reason for that is that searching is concentrated within a particular database or databases dealing with a particular subject, so you are searching a smaller more specialised data set. Also, it is very simple, because of the way the records are structured, to greatly improve precision through use of fields and limits. Most search engines allow you to limit your search to, for example, the URL or the title, but the level of sophistication is poor in comparison to the field searching offered on Dialog. In the library environment, a MARC21 catalogue record is made up of multiple fields: author fields, title fields, date fields, subject headings fields, and so on (see Figure 4.3) – all those fields contain metadata. Full information on the MARC21 formats can be found on the Library of Congress website.[14]

Traditionally published documents contain easily identified metadata. For example, the title page and title page verso of a book contain metadata: that is where you will find the title, the author's name, the publisher and place of publication, the date and so on. This is not necessarily the case with

Figure 4.3 MARC21: outline

Leader and directory
Control fields
Number and code fields
Classification and call number fields
Main entry fields
Title and title-related fields (including author)
Edition, imprint, etc. fields (including publisher)
Physical description etc. fields
Series statement fields
Notes fields
Subject access fields
Added entry fields
Linking entry fields
Series added entry fields
Holdings, location, alternate graphics, etc. fields

web documents; there are no universally applied conventions for web authors to create metadata to describe the contents of their web pages, although we do have a standard (see the section on Dublin Core below). The HTML protocol does not have mandatory resource description sections, but XML, Extensible Markup Language, looks much more promising in terms of record structure and metadata creation.[15]

It is clear that detailed resource description, using metadata, increases the efficiency of retrieval. Users can search for specific attributes like a particular author, date, format and subject, assuming tags and subject descriptors have been assigned to a resource. Essentially, metadata can increase the precision of searching by allowing for sophisticated field searching and subject searching. Subject metadata can also be used to assign resources to a category in a taxonomy, increasing consistency of categorisation and so assisting browsing.

In terms of managing information, some metadata elements are specifically designed for records management. The e-Government metadata standard[16] has an element called 'preservation'. This identifies resources that need to be archived and stored in the long term. In the traditional library environment, all information professionals are familiar with the life cycle of materials – from acquisition through circulation to disposal. Metadata created at the ordering stage is used to manage and track all the other processes.

Rights management, ownership and authenticity are extremely important. Information is a commodity with a real economic value in most organisations. Haynes[17] points out that one of the drivers for the development of metadata standards in the publishing industry has been the need to manage intellectual property rights. Metadata can include information about ownership of intellectual property and information about provenance that can determine the authenticity of a resource and increase its value. This is particularly important in the digital environment, where information can be so easily accessed and reused.

Finally, interoperability and e-commerce is concerned with the exchange of information, sharing of resources and their commercial exploitation. It is useful to provide a formal definition of interoperability: 'Two systems are interoperable if a user of one system can access even some resources or functions of other systems.'[18] This is essentially what the UK e-Government initiative is devised to achieve. Information can flow seamlessly across government departments and can be accessed by the public. Use of the Dublin Core Metadata Element Set and various refinements (explained in detail below) ensures that government websites share a common framework. MARC21[19] is another example – it generates metadata that allow for record sharing between libraries on a global scale. E-commerce depends on the ability to exchange data from one system to another and process it. Again, this is facilitated by a shared framework for managing e-resources.

Dublin Core

As noted above, the UK government uses a modified version of the Dublin Core Metadata Element Set, which is the closest we have to a universally applied standard for metadata creation. Its origins lie in a metadata workshop, organised by OCLC and the National Center for Supercomputer Applications, which was held in Dublin, Ohio in March 1995. Workshop participants included librarians, computer scientists, software developers, publishers and members of the Internet Engineering Task Force, so there was a lot of diversity but the one thing everyone had in common was that they were interested in increasing the efficiency of the search for and retrieval of Internet resources. All participants agreed that any standard metadata would be better than none, anything that might help in selective recovery of information from the Internet.

Participants decided that their goal would be to draft some simple instructions which an author or publisher mounting a document on a network server would be able to use to describe their own resources. The belief was that if it was possible to create a simple standard data element set then it would be possible to encourage authors and publishers to provide metadata with their documents. Standardisation would also allow the developers of web authoring tools to include templates for the metadata in their software. What was also needed was that the set of data elements should be understood across all communities: librarians, computer scientists, publishers, authors. Since 1996 we have had the Dublin Core Metadata Element Set and the move towards its widespread acceptance was helped when the International Organization for Standardization formalised it as a published standard in 2003 (ISO Standard 15836). Dublin Core metadata come somewhere between the crude metadata employed by search engines and the very sophisticated MARC21 formats.

The Dublin Core consists of 15 core elements (see Figure 4.4),[20] which librarians will be pleased to note can be mapped onto existing MARC fields (this is important because libraries will want to catalogue web resources using their existing standards).[21]

Figure 4.4 Dublin Core

Title	The name given to the resource by its creator or publisher.
Creator	The person or persons or organisation primarily responsible for the intellectual content of the resource: authors, illustrators, photographers, artists and so on.
Subject	The topic of the resource or keywords or phrases that describe the subject or content of the resource. The hope is to promote the use of controlled vocabulary here, including Dewey Decimal or Library of Congress class numbers.
Description	A textual description of the content of the resource: an abstract for example.
Publisher	The entity responsible for making the resource available in its present form: a commercial publisher, an organisation, an individual, for example.
Contributors	People or organisations, in addition to those specified in the Creator element, who have made significant contributions to the resource: editors, translators, illustrators and so on.
Date	The date the resource was made available in its current form. The recommended best practice is an eight-digit number: YYYYMMDD.
Type	The category of the resource: for example, homepage, novel, poem, technical report. Resource type should be selected from a designated list.
Format	The data representation of the resource: HTML, PDF, Word, etc. Again it is expected that the format will be selected from a designated list.
Identifier	A string or number used to uniquely identify the resource. For books it would be the ISBN; for web pages it is the URL.
Source	The work, either print or electronic, from which the resource is derived, if applicable.
Language	The language of the intellectual content of the resource. Where practicable the content of this field should be consistent with the standard two- or three-character codes for written languages.
Relation	Relationship to other resources: to provide a means of expressing relationships among resources that have formal relationships to others but which exist as discrete resources themselves.
Coverage	The spatial locations and temporal durations characteristic of the resource: geographic location, period covered.
Rights	A link to a copyright notice of terms of use statement, for example.

One high-profile user of Dublin Core is the UK government. The publication of the 1999 *Modernising Government* White Paper led to the adoption of the Dublin Core metadata standard to improve both internal and public access to electronic resources. It was decided that, although Dublin Core was an excellent starting point, it did not fully cater for specialist needs around records management, data security and the requirements of the Freedom of Information and Data Protection Acts. So, in addition to the 15 Dublin Core elements, more have been added:[22]

- *Accessibility*: the document's physical availability to specific user groups.

- *Addressee*: the person or persons to whom the document was addressed.

- *Aggregation*: the extent to which the document is part of a larger resource.

- *Audience*: who the content of the document is aimed at.

- *Digital signature*: still to be defined.

- *Disposal*: to set a limit on when a document should be updated or removed.

- *Location*: for files held on tape or disk.

- *Mandate*: legislative or other mandate under which the resource was produced.

- *Preservation*: detailed information to ensure files will be readable in the long term.

- *Status*: whether the document is a first or final draft, approved or waiting approval, for example.

As can be seen at the Dublin Core website,[23] the original 15 elements have been refined and added to in an attempt to meet specialised needs. This is, in a sense, unfortunate, as the added complexity may discourage authors from applying the standard. It does, however, allow organisations to tailor the metadata set to their needs, adding elements as appropriate.

We have seen that metadata serve the same purpose as cataloguing in the traditional library environment. Consistently applied rules for resource description are essential in managing documents. Libraries could not function effectively without catalogues; likewise records cannot be managed effectively without metadata. Efficiency is increased by the application of standards which allow for the sharing of metadata both within an organisation and with external agencies. Creators of content can utilise a simple template to assign metadata tags to their documents; this serves to identify individual documents, assists in their retrieval and management, establishes their ownership and authenticity, and enables interoperability. In the next section we concentrate on promoting consistency in how subjects are named and on identifying semantic relationships to increase the efficiency of retrieval.

Thesaurus construction and ontologies

In Chapter 1 we looked at basic principles of indexing and explored the concepts of pre- and post-coordination. Most pre-coordinate subject indexes, where an indexer assigns a series of subject headings to a document, use vocabulary control. In information architecture a taxonomy is essentially a pre-coordinate classified subject index, where vocabulary is controlled by the naming of the subject categories within the taxonomy. When documents are added to the resource their placement within a category will be used in indexing and assigning subject headings. In post-coordinate subject indexes, where terms naming subjects are coordinated by a searcher typing a query in the form of a search statement or phrase, retrieval efficiency can be increased by mapping queries onto a thesaurus that will automatically search for equivalent and associated concepts. Vocabulary control will increase the retrieval efficiency of both the taxonomy and the search engine.

There are basically two agents of vocabulary control: subject headings lists and thesauri. Rowley says that they both have the same functions:

- to control terminology used in indexes; and
- to control the display of relationships between concepts in indexes.[24]

Subject headings lists are alphabetical lists of subject terms that have been specified for use in an index, a catalogue or a database for describing subjects. A subject headings list will contain both approved and non-approved headings (synonyms) as entry points. It will generally include qualifiers for homographs (same word but different meanings: rooks, birds; rooks, chessmen) it will generally include compound headings made up of multiple words or phrases, and it will include referencing to indicate relationships between terms. To further illustrate the theoretical principles and structure of subject headings lists, it is useful to briefly examine two of the best known: Sears and Library of Congress. The Sears List of Subject Headings controls indexing language by:

- *specifying terms that can be used to describe subjects*;
- *specifying preferred word form*, following the well established convention that plural nouns are preferred: diseases rather than disease;
- *using referencing to eliminate synonyms and to link associated concepts*: 'use' references for synonyms (equivalent to 'see' references), 'RT' (related term) references for associated concepts (equivalent to 'see also' references);
- *specifying the use of various forms of subdivision*: by subject, form, period and location, for example.

Rowley says that Sears employs three basic principles:

- *use of specific rather than broad headings* – increases precision of naming;
- *use of popular rather than technical terminology* – promotes the widest understanding of concepts;
- *use of consistency in application of subject headings* – an attempt is made to offer one heading, and only one heading, for each concept.[25]

Much more detailed than Sears, and sharing the features noted above, is the Library of Congress Subject Headings. The listing contains the complete subject entry vocabulary of the Library of Congress catalogues and is under constant revision. It is important to note that subject headings lists are not static; as terminology changes, these changes have to be reflected in the agents of vocabulary control. It is interesting to see how the LCSH vocabulary is evolving, with frequent deletions, additions and modifications noted in 'Weekly lists'.[26] Given that subject headings lists exist to promote consistency, it is worrying to note that it is possible to identify inconsistencies, even in widely used authority lists like Sears and Library of Congress. Practical points to note when naming and presenting concepts are as follows:

- *Make sure that headings represent complex or specific subjects accurately*. It is important to be as specific as possible when describing concepts.
- *Make sure that headings are selected and constructed systematically*. For example, be consistent in use of word form and in whether or not compound headings are inverted: 'Pre-coordinate indexes' or 'Indexes: pre-coordinate'.

- *Always be systematic in constructing references.* Make sure that appropriately detailed references are included for synonymous terms and, equally important, make sure that completely redundant references are not included.

The general principles and guidelines pertaining to subject headings lists also apply in the creation of the second agent of vocabulary control, to be considered in the next section: the thesaurus.

Thesauri

Its Wikipedia entry defines a thesaurus as: 'A list of every important term (single-word or multi-word) in a given domain of knowledge; and a set of related terms for every term in the list.'[27] The primary function of a thesaurus is to show semantic relationships between terms: relationships based on their meaning; it is what a classification scheme does, but with terms arranged alphabetically instead of notationally. The thesaurus is also, like a subject headings list, an authority list showing terms that may and may not be used in an index. Thesauri tend to concentrate on specific subject areas: examples are the Thesaurus of Psychological Index Terms, the Medical Subject Headings, the Inspec thesaurus for physics and electronics, the ERIC thesaurus for education and related fields, the ASSIA thesaurus for the social sciences, and so on.

Using a thesaurus you will see under each heading or descriptor various words or abbreviations used to clarify meaning or indicate relationships with other terms. The most common are explained in Figure 4.5.

So in a thesaurus there are a series of headings that serve to control vocabulary, and under each heading is displayed its relationship to other headings in the list.

Thesaurus construction

It is appropriate to examine thesaurus construction in some depth because the preliminary stages are essentially the same as the early stages of taxonomy creation, involving subject analysis and classification. However, it is important to stress that the finished thesaurus is not the same as the taxonomy as presented on the system interface. The thesaurus is essentially an agent of vocabulary control; it will include terms that will not be present in the taxonomy. The thesaurus is arranged

Figure 4.5 Thesaurus entries: abbreviations and relationships

SN Scope note

A definition note: a sentence or short paragraph that defines a heading

UF Use for

Indicating the heading is the preferred term. For example:
Businesses
UF Firms
Of course if the user looked under 'Firms' they would find a complementary reference:
Firms
USE Businesses

BT Broader term

Used to link the heading to others one level higher up in the hierarchy of relationships. For example:
Drama
BT Arts

NT Narrower term

Used to link the heading to others one level lower down in the hierarchy of relationships. For example:
Arts
NT Art
Drama
Literature
Music
Performing Arts

RT Related term

Used to link the heading to others on the same level in the hierarchy of relationships. For example:
Drama
RT Performing Arts

and presented alphabetically; the taxonomy may be arranged and presented conceptually, sequentially and/or alphabetically. Nevertheless, the principles of thesaurus construction can be applied in taxonomy construction, and as we will see when we focus on ontologies, can add considerable value to both the taxonomy and the system's search engine.

At the start of the process there are a number of issues that need to be addressed. The first thing to consider is obviously the subject field. What are the boundaries of the subject? What are the core areas requiring depth treatment? What are the marginal areas which need to be present but which can have a more superficial treatment? In conjunction with this you ought to consider the system users: who are they? You should already have established this in the needs, task and resource analysis. Importantly the system users will determine the type of terminology you use in your thesaurus and in your taxonomy. You should find out from them how they name the various concepts that need to be included. The next series of questions relate to specificity and depth of indexing. How will the system be used? What kind of information will users need? What kind of searches will users conduct? If detailed and specific information is needed, then the thesaurus and the taxonomy will have to achieve that level of specificity.

So, in the early stages of thesaurus construction there are three basic things that need to be established:

- the scope of the subject area;
- how your users name subjects;
- the level of detail required.

Next, consideration should be given to controlling the terminology. The thesaurus as an agent of vocabulary control can point users to preferred terms; a taxonomy should include only the preferred terms. Consistency in use of word form is important as has already been noted: are singular or plural forms used? Plurals are generally preferred, but common sense should prevail. In the case of nouns it is useful to differentiate between count nouns and non-count nouns. Count nouns are subject to the question 'how many?': how many lawyers, how many scientists, how many women, how many substances, how many investments – they are usually expressed as plurals. Non-count nouns are subject to the question 'how much?': how much electricity, how much waste, how much steel, how much work. But, of course, some nouns can also be verbs depending on how the term is being applied: how much investment. So although you can use the principle of count and non-count nouns as a general rule it is still important to use common sense and aim for the greatest level of consistency.

Consideration should be given to how compound terms are expressed. Compound terms will need to be included because a lot of subjects can only be expressed as a phrase, and even when that is not the case a compound term will reduce ambiguity and increase specificity. Consistency in whether compound headings are inverted or not is important: 'user models' or 'models: users', 'hazardous substances' or 'substances: hazardous', and so on. The thesaurus can also contain scope notes or definitions of terms as another way to reduce ambiguity. These would not appear in the taxonomy, but the classified or conceptual arrangement there should help to reduce ambiguity.

When the terminology has been established, relationships can be identified. There are three types of relationships of interest here:

- *Equivalence relationships.* Some of the terms representing subjects might be synonymous, they mean the same thing. In that case only one of those synonymous terms should be used as a heading. That means that the other terms will be entry points in the thesaurus to allow for different ways in which users might describe the same concept, and will be linked to the preferred term by means of USE references. Only the term used as a heading will be included in the taxonomy which obviously helps to reduce size and complexity.

- *Hierarchical relationships showing levels of superordination and subordination.* A superordinate term represents a class and the subordinate terms refer to its members. So basically here you are looking for broader and narrower concepts in a logically progressive sequence.

- *Associative relationships.* These are terms which are conceptually related. Here it is not possible to identify a hierarchical relationship and terms would be linked with RT or Related Term references.

Having decided on the subjects that need to be present and how they are to be expressed, and having identified relationships, you are ready to construct the thesaurus. The relationships that have been identified with the broader and narrower terms can obviously be used to determine the structure of the hierarchy as represented in a taxonomy.

Principles of thesaurus construction and how a thesaurus differs from a taxonomy can be illustrated by using part of the Dewey schedules.[28] The Dewey Decimal Classification schedules are structured like a taxonomy: they display a series of hierarchical relationships as shown in Appendix 1.

Dewey's ordering of Regional Medicine as displayed in the classified sequence is literally top-down. In a thesaurus the listing of subjects would not be conceptual or logical, it would be strictly alphabetical. So the first thing to do in creating a thesaurus based on this part of the Dewey schedule is to create an alphabetical listing (see Appendix 2). We can also, at this point, start to indicate equivalence or synonymous relationships. This listing could be improved upon; singular nouns are used rather than plurals (except for hernias). Also, American spellings are applied throughout and this would need to be amended. In practice, headings would have greater consistency, but the language of the DDC schedules is retained here.

You would now proceed by taking one term at a time and listing under it all the terms which have some relationship to it (see Appendix 3). The relationships are derived directly from the DDC hierarchy. RT or related term has only been used for areas of the body that are (roughly) adjacent to each other or that share obvious similarities.

You can see from Appendix 3 how at each entry in the thesaurus you have displayed its relationships to other headings. The list is very long, much longer than the original classified and alphabetical headings listings, but has been somewhat shortened by using synonymous terms as entry points with USE references rather than displaying the hierarchy of relationships under every term. The display of relationships is much more detailed than you would find in a subject headings list.

So far the focus has been upon thesauri in general terms. Now it is appropriate to concentrate on two in particular, the Inspec thesaurus[29] and the ERIC thesaurus,[30] as they have features that make them good exemplars in the context of information architecture and taxonomy creation. The Inspec thesaurus is used to index the Inspec database produced by the Institution of Engineering and Technology, and is the major abstracting service for physics, electronics, communications, electrical engineering, information technology and computing. The thesaurus is in two parts: the alphabetical list of terms and the list of term trees. As well as the usual BT, NT and RT links, every heading in the thesaurus also includes a TT link. In our 'Regional Medicine' example the TT (top term in the hierarchy) would be Medicine. The Inspec thesaurus's term tree listing is an alphabetical list of top terms with all their narrower concepts listed beneath them. So, for example, under the top term medicine would appear, along, of course, with lots of other entries, the listing shown in Appendix 4.

The structure here is like a taxonomy, but with a purely alphabetical arrangement rather than conceptual or logical. 'Medicine' is the equivalent of the main class or top-level category, it is the broadest term. Then we move down a level in the hierarchy to 'Regional medicine', then down another level to concepts like 'Abdominal and pelvic cavities', and continue to a lower level that includes concepts like 'Intestine' and so on.

These examples show how the same information can be presented in various ways: traditional classification scheme, alphabetical subject headings list, thesaurus, taxonomy. The ERIC thesaurus for education and related fields produced by the Educational Resources Information Center can be used to illustrate yet another way to express relationships between subjects. Its main alphabetical listing of terms includes the usual BT, NT and RT references, additionally each preferred term or heading includes details of its Group Code (GC). This refers to the ERIC Descriptor Groups: all the terms in the thesaurus are allocated to nine broad groups, which are in turn divided into 41 smaller groups. Some of these smaller groups contain over 200 terms. This is a very useful feature – the descriptor groups provide an extra level of detail, showing terms that are not necessarily closely related but which are in the same general subject area. Referring to the descriptor groups can help indexers by suggesting alternative headings and it can help searchers by suggesting alternative terms to use to broaden the scope of their search.

So far in this section the focus has been mainly upon traditional uses of thesauri. A more detailed consideration must now be given to how a thesaurus would be used in the digital environment. Rosenfeld and Morville[31] suggest thesauri can be utilised in one of three ways and differentiate between: an indexing thesaurus, a searching thesaurus and a classic thesaurus. Each of these requires further explanation. An indexing thesaurus simply allows for consistency of naming when documents are being added to the resource, which is important in promoting shared understanding of terminology. Users could check the indexing thesaurus to help them select keywords to use in searching. A searching thesaurus, Rosenfeld and Morville suggest, would not be used for indexing, perhaps because the volume of documentation is too great to allow for manual indexing, but it could be used to improve the efficiency of searching. When a user inputs a key term, it would be mapped against the thesaurus which would then automatically expand the query by searching under all equivalent (synonymous) and associated terms in the database. This would greatly enhance the effectiveness of natural language searches in a full-text database. A classic thesaurus has a lot in common with an ontology, which is examined in greater detail below. A classic thesaurus would be available to assist in the indexing of individual documents when they are being added to the system: selection of an index term by an indexer would automatically assign all related terms to the document. Also, when someone searches for documents using simple keyword queries, the query would be automatically matched with all the related concepts, thus eliminating synonyms and retrieving concepts that have associative and hierarchical relationships. The classic thesaurus is the most powerful: a fully integrated indexing, search and retrieval tool.

Ontology

A dictionary definition of ontology is 'the branch of metaphysics that deals with the nature and essence of things or of existence'.[32] This is not particularly useful and helps to confuse rather than to clarify. Gruber's commonly cited definition of an ontology as 'a specification of a conceptualisation'[33] places it within the discipline of knowledge and information management rather than philosophy but does little to explain its meaning. A more detailed definition places ontology firmly within the context of classification and thesaurus construction: 'An ontology is a document or file that formally defines the relations among terms. The most typical kind of ontology for the web has a taxonomy and a set of inference rules.'[34] As has already been noted, a taxonomy consists of the hierarchical display of a series of classes and sub-classes. The inference rules in an ontology basically add value and sophistication to a taxonomy. This is also what the classic thesaurus does.

An example of an inference rule using the animal kingdom taxonomy from Chapter 1 would be: If X belongs in the subphylum Y, and Z is an X, then Z also belongs in the subphylum Y. A specific instance would be: If a mammal belongs in the subphylum Vertebrata, and a dog is a mammal, then a dog also belongs in the subphylum Vertebrata. An example using the DDC schedules would be: If 617.55 is the class number for 'Abdominal and pelvic cavities' and 'Intestine' has the class number 617.554, then 'Intestine' must be part of 'Abdominal and pelvic cavities'. The inclusion of inference rules would allow a system to support hierarchically expanded searching: if the user is interested in this concept, then they would probably be interested in these related concepts.

The power of the ontology can be increased further with the inclusion of equivalence relationships. Examples might be: TV is equivalent to Television; Chest is equivalent to Thorax. When a user is searching for information the equivalence relationship would map the user's query onto other terms representing the same concept, dispensing with the need for the user to specify synonymous terms in a search statement.

Essentially, inference rules serve the same purpose as a hierarchically structured classification scheme or thesaurus, making explicit how concepts are logically related to each other. Equivalence relationships basically serve the same purpose as *see* or *use* references in an index or thesaurus to control vocabulary and eliminate synonyms. The concept of an ontology may seem unfamiliar to librarians, but in fact it is intimately related to classification and thesaurus construction. Soergel makes this very clear when he writes of ontologies: 'A classification by any other name is still a classification.'[35]

So why is this important? We have already seen that thesaurus construction is very similar to taxonomy construction: identifying hierarchical and associative relationships. We have also looked at the importance of vocabulary control and the identification of equivalence relationships. A taxonomy is essentially a browsing interface to a collection of e-documents, but any effective retrieval system must be capable of being searched as well as browsed. This is really where we can appreciate the power of the classic thesaurus or the ontology. Classification schemes and thesauri are essentially knowledge representations: they attempt to create knowledge structures. An ontology has also been described as a knowledge representation: it allows search software to go beyond keyword matching and specify the meaning of concepts, their semantics. It does this by assigning concepts to classes and defining their properties based on the class they are located within. This actually has a lot in common with faceted classification. A faceted classification scheme for music recordings might include facets for: Artist: Album: Genre. Each of those facets or classes would contain a list of individual instances with associated properties. For example, Artist is Scritti Politti, Album is White Bread, Black Beer, Genre (according to iTunes) is Alternative. So Scritti Politti has the property of Artist and Alternative. White Bread, Black Beer has the property of being Alternative and an Album by Scritti Politti. Anyone searching for Scritti Politti would retrieve information about White Bread, Black Beer and an indication that they might be interested in other Alternative artists. This is a very simple example but it illustrates how the conceptual relationships defined by an ontology allow the searcher to retrieve potentially relevant information that is not solely dependent on the presence of keywords.

Another example, based on our thesaurus structure for regional medicine, would be: a searcher types the word 'Chest'; the ontology recognises that 'Chest' is equivalent to 'Thorax'; recognising the equivalence relationship, as well as retrieving items associated with the terms 'Thorax' and 'Chest', suggests that associated concepts like lungs and ribs might be of interest. This is making full use of the thesaurus's conceptual representation – by mapping the user's query onto narrower terms.

This has implications for information systems within organisations; it also, of course, has implications for information systems generally. Berners-Lee states that ontologies are a basic component of the Semantic Web.[36] The Semantic Web will rely upon structured collections of information and sets of inference rules to allow software agents to support human searchers. The sort of knowledge representations we are familiar with in the forms of classification schemes (including taxonomies) and thesauri can provide the backbone of this technology.

Summary

In this chapter the focus has been upon documents and document description. We have seen that content – information that has been described, structured and organised – is at the heart of any information system. Individual documents may contain many individual content components or records. Documents have to be analysed and described, using standard metadata, and their content components have to be identified, mapped and managed. Vocabulary control in describing content and identification of equivalence and associative relationships among subjects as seen in thesauri has the potential to greatly increase the efficiency of taxonomies and search engines.

Further reading

For all aspects of content, content management and content management systems, Boiko's book provides detailed and in-depth coverage (over one thousand pages):

- Boiko, B. (2005) *Content Management Bible*, 2nd edn. Indianapolis, IN: Wiley.

Haynes provides good, detailed coverage of metadata:

- Haynes, D. (2004) *Metadata for Information Management and Retrieval*. London: Facet.

The Dublin Core website is also recommended; as well as the Metadata Element Set and its extensions, there is a lot of documentation relating to the standard and to metadata generally:

- *http://dublincore.org*

The best source of information about MARC21 is the Library of Congress website:

- *http://www.loc.gov/marc/*

Although not cited in the references, a detailed introduction to thesaurus construction is provided in the classic text:

- Aitchison, J. et al (2000) *Thesaurus Construction and Use: A Practical Manual*, 4th edn. London: Aslib.

Anyone wishing to explore the concept of the Semantic Web should read Tim Berners-Lee's article for *Scientific American*:

- Berners-Lee, T. et al. (2001) 'The Semantic Web', *Scientific American*, 17 May. Available at: *http://www.scientificamerican.com/article.cfm? articleID=00048144-10D2-1C70-84A9809EC588EF21&catID=2* (accessed 10 August 2006).

There is also useful background information at the W3C website:

- *http://www.w3.org/2001/sw/*

References

1. Boiko, B. (2005) *Content Management Bible*, 2nd edn. Indianapolis, IN: Wiley, pp. 8–9.
2. Association of Records Managers and Administrators (1989) *Glossary of Records Management Terms*. Prairie Village, KS: ARMA International.
3. Association of Records Managers and Administrators: *http://www .arma.org/erecords/index.cfm* (accessed 2 August 2006).
4. Schwartz, C. and Hernon, P. (1993) *Records Management in the Library*. Norwood, NJ: Ablex.
5. Rosenfeld, L. and Morville, P. (2002) *Information Architecture for the World Wide Web*, 2nd edn. Sebastopol, CA: O'Reilly, p. 221.
6. Ibid.
7. Boiko, op. cit., p. 591.
8. Ibid., pp. 563–4.
9. Rosenfeld and Morville, op. cit., p. 289.

10. Ibid., p. 290.

11. Ibid., p. 296.

12. Vellucci, S. (1998) 'Metadata', *ARIST*, 33: 187–222.

13. Haynes, D. (2004) *Metadata for Information Management and Retrieval*. London: Facet, pp. 15–17.

14. Library of Congress (2005) *MARC standards*: *http://www.loc.gov/marc/* (accessed 9 August 2006).

15. W3C, *Extensible Markup Language*: *http://www.w3.org/XML/* (accessed 3 August 2006).

16. *e-Government metadata standard: version 3.0* (2004): *http://www.govtalk.gov.uk/schemasstandards/metadata_document.asp?docnum=872* (accessed 3 August 2006).

17. Haynes, op. cit., p. 118.

18. Shirky, C. (2001) *Interoperability, Not Standards*, available at: *http://www.openp2p.com/pub/a/p2p/2001/03/15/clay_interop.html* (accessed 3 August 2006).

19. Library of Congress (2005) *MARC21 concise format for bibliographic data*: *http://www.loc.gov/marc/bibliographic/* (accessed 3 August 2006).

20. Dublin Core Metadata Initiative (2004) *Dublin Core Metadata Element Set, version 1.1*: reference description: *http://dublincore.org/documents/dces/* (accessed 3 August 2006).

21. Library of Congress (2005) *MARC21 formats: MARC mappings*: *http://www.loc.gov/marc/marcdocz.html* (accessed 9 August 2006).

22. *e-Government metadata standard: version 3.0*, op. cit.

23. Dublin Core Metadata Initiative (2006) *Other Elements and Element Refinements*: *http://dublincore.org/documents/dcmi-terms/#H3* (accessed 3 August 2006).

24. Rowley, J.E. (1992) *Organizing Knowledge*, 2nd edn. Aldershot: Gower, p. 242.

25. Ibid., pp. 244–5.

26. Library of Congress (2006) *Library of Congress Subject Headings: Weekly lists*: *http://www.loc.gov/catdir/cpso/cpso.html#subjects* (accessed 9 August 2006).

27. Thesaurus: *http://en.wikipedia.org/wiki/Thesaurus* (accessed 7 August 2006).

28. *Dewey Decimal Classification*, 22nd edn (2003) Dublin, OH: OCLC.

29. *Inspec thesaurus*, London: Institution of Engineering and Technology.

30. ERIC thesaurus: *http://www.eric.ed.gov/ERICWebPortal/Home .portal?_nfpb=true&_pageLabel=Thesaurus&_nfls=false* (accessed 7 August 2006).
31. Rosenfeld and Morville, op. cit., pp. 193–6.
32. *Chambers 21st Century Dictionary* (1999) Edinburgh: Chambers.
33. Gruber, T.R. (1993) 'A translation approach to portable ontologies', *Knowledge Acquisition*, 5 (2): 199–220.
34. Berners-Lee, T. et al. (2001) 'The semantic web', *Scientific American*, 17 May.
35. Soergel, D. (1999) 'The rise of ontologies or the reinvention of classification', *Journal of the American Society for Information Science*, 50 (12): 1119–20.
36. Berners-Lee et al., op. cit.

Interface and display design

Preece et al. state:

> For computers to be widely accepted and used effectively they need
> to be well designed. This is not to say that all systems have to be
> designed to accommodate everyone, but that computers should be
> designed for the needs and capabilities of the people for whom they
> are intended.[1]

In this chapter we concentrate, not on the computer per se, but rather on
the design of the interface and the aesthetic appeal of the resource in an
exploration of basic concepts of user-centred design. Users of a system
need to be able to extract information quickly and to navigate the
information architecture efficiently. This means that the interface should
be well organised, well laid out and make effective use of graphics and
colour. This is a very obvious point to make, but in practice it is all too
easily forgotten. Norman reminds us that: 'One side effect of today's
technologically advanced world is that it is not uncommon to hate the
things we interact with.'[2] It is interesting that he uses the term 'hate'.
Shneiderman prefers anger: 'The first step toward the new computing will
be to promote good design by getting angry about the quality of user
interfaces and the underlying infrastructure.'[3] People can experience a
strong emotional reaction to technology and its artefacts. In Chapter 2
you were introduced to Kuhlthau's 'affect' realm[4] which reminds us that
how people feel plays an important part in task completion; it is certain
that an aesthetically appealing and well organised resource will elicit a
positive emotional response from users. As will be discussed later in this
chapter, display design can evoke strong feelings – we immediately like or
dislike a website on the basis of the colours and graphics and the screen
layout. This immediate response can determine whether or not we explore
the site further. Tidwell[5] points out that the Stanford Web Credibility

Project[6] found that the most important factor determining whether people trust or distrust websites was the appearance of the website, whether it looked professional and was well designed. Appearance actually outweighed factors like company reputation and customer service: the art and science of interface design should not be underestimated.

In practice an organisation will probably have two interfaces to its information resources: one for staff (intranet) and one for the public (extranet). Nielsen points out that: 'For intranet designs, efficiency, memorability, and error reduction become the most important usability attributes.'[7] This is an important point to make; it reminds us that the needs of the user have to be considered at all times. General design principles apply to both intranets and extranets, but intranets serve a different purpose and can support denser content. Extranets have to appeal to the widest possible audience, have to convey positive messages about the organisation and serve as devices to advertise and promote products or services.

So first impressions and the appeal and professionalism of the screen design are extremely important, but the aesthetic quality of the display design is just one aspect of the problem. Other related factors will affect the usability of the resource, and it is those factors we examine first.

The human-computer interface

Examining HCI issues in systems design will provide a foundation to the elements of display design we will examine later. The study of HCI allows us to take a more formal approach to thinking about interaction and the system interface. HCI (human-computer interaction or human-computer interface) is an acronym rarely used in the literature in recent years, having been largely superseded by HII (human-information interaction) but it actually represents the subject of interest very well. As the name suggests, HCI is the study of the interaction between humans and computers. It is concerned with designing computer systems which take account of the needs of the people who use them – so it is broader in scope than interface design and is obviously at the heart of user-centred design.

Although interest in HCI as a discipline developed throughout the 1980s, it cannot be assumed that its principles are firmly embedded in the systems being developed today. In the 1980s computer companies exploited the term 'user-friendly' which, in practice, often meant tidying up screen displays to make them more aesthetically pleasing. Academic researchers focused on the 'people side' of interaction with computer systems, often concentrating on the psychology of interaction. One of the aims of HCI research was to improve interface design based upon an understanding of system users.

Definitions of HCI are very broad. For example:

> Human-computer interaction is a discipline concerned with the design, evaluation and implementation of interactive computing systems for human use and with the study of major phenomena surrounding them.[8]

> Human-computer interaction (HCI) or, alternatively, man-machine interaction (MMI) or computer-human interaction (symbolized as X Chi the 22nd letter of the Greek alphabet) is the study of interaction between people (users) and computers. It is an interdisciplinary subject, relating computer science with many other fields of study and research.[9]

Any definition of HCI will basically confirm that it is about people using computers and that its goal is to assist in designing computer systems that people can use – which very often means designing the interface to the system in a way that takes account of the needs of the users.

Just as definitions of HCI are broad, so too, as suggested in the second definition cited above, is its scope. Booth[10] suggests that ten major disciplines play a role within HCI:

- *Ergonomics or human factors* – the study and design of the physical characteristics of computer workstations: designing keyboards that will reduce the risk of repetitive strain injury, optimising screen size, and so on.

- *Software engineering* – providing new tools to improve interaction and manage and control the design process.

- *Mathematics* – used to assess the cognitive complexity of a task or interface, for example. Basically using quantitative methods to analyse the human–computer interface.

- *Cognitive psychology* – the scientific analysis of human mental processes and structures. Its aim is to understand human behaviour. A lot of what cognitive psychology has learned about human information processing and behaviour is relevant to HCI and will be explored in this chapter.

- *Artificial intelligence* – AI research has developed cognitive models that can represent the user. A lot of AI research is focused on trying to model intelligence and it also offers the possibility of intelligent systems – systems that might adapt to the needs of a particular user, for example.

- *Computational linguistics* – having its origins in the work of Chomsky its contribution to HCI is in understanding the dialogue that goes on at the interface and in developing natural language systems.

- *Cognitive science* – aiming to understand and explain higher cognitive processes such as understanding, thought and creativity. One of cognitive science's major contributions to HCI is the concept of mental models explained later in this chapter.

- *Social psychology.*

- *Organisational psychology.*

- *Sociology.*

The final three concepts are concerned with understanding the impact of computer systems – resistance to change, acceptance, and so on. Essentially dealing with pre- and post-design issues, social psychology and organisational psychology are important in needs analysis, for example.

It is certainly not appropriate to discuss all of the above here. We have, to some extent, already examined aspects of social and organisation psychology in Chapter 2. Also in that chapter, we looked at some elements of cognitive psychology in our examination of needs and resource analysis. At this point, because our concern is user-centred design, it is useful to explore the psychology of interaction in more depth by focusing on some of the contributions HCI research has made in understanding the cognitive aspects of computer use.

Mental models and metaphors

> In interacting with the environment, with others, and with the artefacts of technology, people form internal, mental models of themselves and of the things with which they are interacting. These models provide predictive and explanatory power for understanding the interaction.[11]

When people interact with something for the first time they do so within the framework of a mental model based on their existing knowledge and experience. If the mental model is accurate then the interaction has a successful outcome. The power of mental models is that they help people to respond appropriately in unfamiliar situations. In the context of HCI a mental model will incorporate user beliefs and expectations and knowledge of system capabilities based on previous interaction with it and other systems. Lidwell et al. point out that in systems design there are two types of mental models: 'mental models of how systems work (system models) and mental models of how people interact with systems (interaction models)'.[12] Systems designers will have complete and accurate system models; users will have interaction models of varying completeness and accuracy.

Good user-centred design involves matching the system model to the interaction model. If there is a match between the user's mental model and the system model, completion of tasks within a novel environment can be mastered quickly and successfully. An obvious example of incorporating a user's mental model in system design is in the correspondence between the physical office and the virtual desktop, with the virtual documents being represented as though they were paper: capable of being typed, filed in folders and put in the bin for recycling. Commonly though, a user approaching a system for the first time may bring an inappropriate mental model with them, or at least one that does not match the system model. For example, students often mistakenly assume that they interact with an information retrieval system like Dialog in the same way that they interact with a web search engine like Google. Something people do very well is to use a small amount of knowledge to infer a great deal.

One approach designers adopt to make sure that computer users acquire an appropriate mental model of a system is to provide metaphors. Lakoff and Johnson state that: 'The essence of metaphor is understanding and experiencing one kind of thing in terms of another.'[13] Metaphors help people to understand something new and unfamiliar by describing it in familiar terms – so they can draw on prior knowledge or experience to help them comprehend something new. This sort of link to existing knowledge helps people to develop appropriate mental models of something they have not experienced before.

So a metaphor is a way of rationalising something we do not understand by comparing it with something we do understand. One of the first computer companies to realise the potential of designing interfaces to be more like the physical world people are familiar with was Xerox. They designed an interface metaphor that was based on the physical office – the Star user interface, launched in 1982. This was the basis of the now familiar WIMP (window, icon, mouse, pointer (or pull-down menu)) environment. Office objects were portrayed as icons on the screen – paper, folders, filing cabinets, etc. The overall organising metaphor that was presented on the screen was of a desk in an office. We are all so familiar with this desktop metaphor now that it is difficult to imagine interacting with a computer without it.

Because metaphors are so powerful and so easily digested, designers must be sure that they use them correctly in design, or else they can cause more problems than they solve. The use of icons as metaphors for functions can be used as an example. Not everyone will understand the connection between the icon and the function it represents.

What about the Microsoft Word toolbar as shown in Figure 5.1 – do all those icons make sense? Most of us will be very familiar with Word and we will have learned the functionality of the various icons, often by moving the pointer over them to reveal the text labels, but they are not immediately obvious.

The Internet Explorer toolbar does rather better (see Figure 5.2), but then there are fewer icons, the icons are larger and the selective use of text labels rids them of any ambiguity.

Figure 5.1 Microsoft Word toolbar

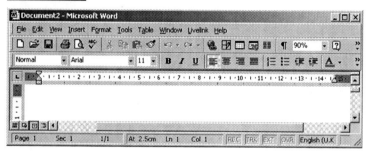

Figure 5.2 Internet Explorer toolbar

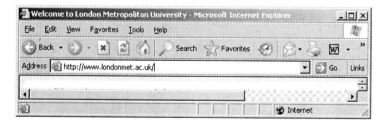

So icons as metaphors can help users by representing system functions in a way that is familiar to them, helping them to develop an appropriate mental model of the system. Designing icons is actually a very difficult thing to do well – a pictogram that seems to have an obvious meaning to one person may be misinterpreted by others. If you decide that it would be desirable to have icons as shortcuts to applications or services and so on, then as with any other aspect of systems design various solutions should be tested and evaluated.

Interaction styles

There are various ways in which users can input and extract data. Often a system interface will provide for a range of different interaction styles depending on the nature of the task and the capabilities of the user. Different interaction styles will accommodate different levels of user expertise – remember the novice or first-time user, the knowledgeable intermittent user and the expert user from the model we looked at in Chapter 2.

The earliest way of communicating with a computer was by typing in commands. The advantages of this approach are: it is powerful, flexible and it appeals to expert users. The main disadvantage is that it usually requires a lot of training and memorising of the various commands. Most users will not have to master a command language in order to interact with systems today, but a command interface can provide expert users with a level of control that is difficult to replicate in other forms of interaction. Regular users of Dialog value the greater precision and control that the command mode gives them, allowing them to search for and retrieve information with a speed and efficiency that is not provided for in the more user-friendly guided search mode.

Dialog offers two command interfaces: DialogWeb and Dialog Classic (see Figures 5.3 and 5.4). The DialogWeb interface is certainly more appealing, but the expert will use the same commands in both the Web and Classic versions.

An alternative system, which is much better for the non-expert, is the menu-driven interface. In this mode of interaction you do not have to remember what you want; you simply have to recognise it. This approach is useful for novice or intermittent users and it also of course emphasises the importance of designing icons or naming menu items which are self-explanatory – not as easy as it might at first seem. You will

Figure 5.3 Dialog Classic command interface

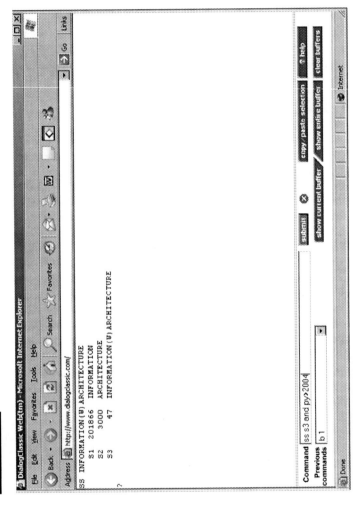

Figure 5.4 DialogWeb command interface

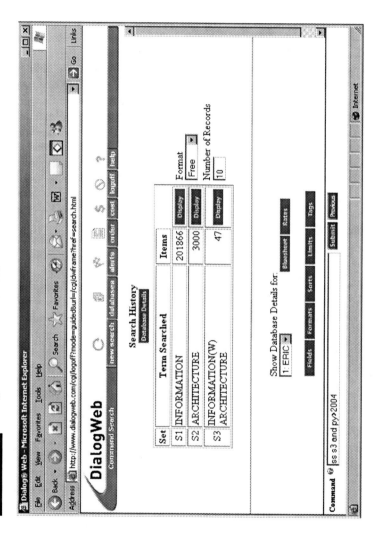

also be familiar with solutions to the problem of making room for all the menu options available – drop-down and pop-up menus. The advantages of this approach are: it shortens the learning process (reducing cognitive effort), it reduces the number of keystrokes needed to perform a function (reducing physical effort) and it structures decision-making which can help users to develop appropriate mental models of the information space. The disadvantages are: you can have too many menus which make the interface look cluttered and selection from a series of menus can be slow for frequent users.

Web directories offer a menu-based approach to search and retrieval (see Figure 5.5). As we explored in Chapter 3 on searching and finding, this can be a quick and efficient way to retrieve web resources.

The form-fill mode of interaction was an early development designed for clerical workers with minimal computing experience to carry out repetitive data input and collection tasks. These interfaces mimicked paper forms. This type of interface is still widely used and can help novice users. For example, the 'Advanced Search' facilities in some search engines like Google and AltaVista use form filling. It is also commonly applied when users have to input personal details (name, address, telephone number, e-mail address, payment details) when ordering goods and services online. The advantages are that it simplifies data entry and minimal training is required. The disadvantages are that it will slow down expert users and it can use up a lot of screen space.

The Expedia.co.uk site has form-filling on its homepage to help users who enter the site to book their trip rather than to browse (see Figure 5.6). Very often form-filling is used after goods have been selected for purchase.

Another style of interaction is through natural language dialogue. Here the system needs to be able to cope with the potentially vague, ambiguous and ungrammatical way users will frame requests. Search engines like Ask use this approach and systems now do rather well in picking out key terms from queries input in natural language. The advantage of using natural language is that users do not have to learn complicated syntax, so again it is an approach that appeals to the novice user. The main disadvantage is that it can still be rather unpredictable. Reliance on natural language in information search and retrieval, although helpful for novice users, does mean that users develop poor search skills. If a search for information is unsuccessful they may not have alternative strategies to apply to the problem.

A final approach to be explored here is the direct manipulation system as represented by the WIMP interface. The concept of direct manipulation

Figure 5.5 Open Directory

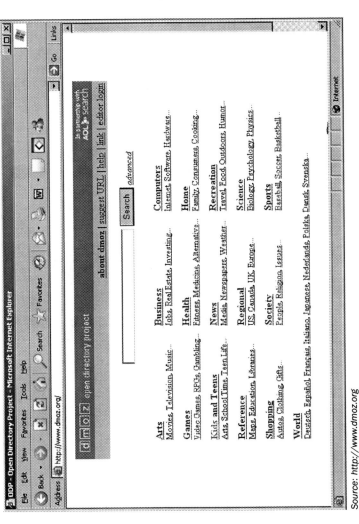

Figure 5.6 Expedia.co.uk: home page

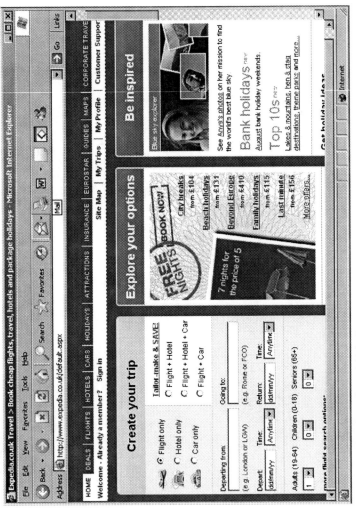

Source: http://www.expedia.co.uk/default.aspx

refers to the fact that the user can interact with metaphorical objects on the screen as if they were the real objects and, importantly, get immediate feedback about their actions. Ideally, there should be no perceivable delay between user input and system response. If this is achieved, the interface itself becomes transparent and the user seems to deal directly with the objects they are manipulating.

Hutchins et al.[14] developed a framework that characterised directness in terms of two gulfs which describe the gap between the users' goals and the system image. The degree of directness in direct manipulation interfaces can be thought of as the distance between the two gulfs: the gulf of execution and the gulf of evaluation. The distance relates to the potential mismatch that can occur between the way a person thinks about a task and the way it is represented by the system – just as in the interaction models and system models explained earlier. The key concern is finding ways to reduce the discrepancy between the users' goals and the system's physical state and form. By reducing the gap, the mismatch between the users' way of thinking about their tasks and the system's representation of them is reduced – so making it easier for users to carry out their tasks. Designers try to bridge the two gulfs, either by changing the users' goals and interpretation of the system, or by changing the input or output aspects of the system. In user-centred design the aim is to match the input and output characteristics of the system to the users' expectations – so increasing the directness of the interaction.

Because all websites use the direct manipulation interface, it is useful to explore elements of its design in more detail.

Basic design principles

Norman[15] sets out a list of design principles for everyday objects. It is obviously the case that bad design does not only apply to websites and you will find some classic examples from toothpaste tubes to CD players at Bad Human Factors Designs.[16] Some of these are very amusing, but there is a serious point, and principles of good (and bad) design also apply to direct manipulation interfaces. The primary design principles are:

- *Affordances*. The design of, for example, an icon should suggest or afford its functionality. Doors afford opening, but does the design of the door suggest it should be pushed or pulled open? A scroll bar is a good example – the box moving up and down through the shaft mimics moving up and down through a document. The shaft suggests that the box can be moved up and down, that it affords vertical movement.

- *Constraints.* Affordances suggest what an object can do and how we interact with it. Constraints limit the number of possibilities of what can be done with it. Norman[17] suggests there are four main types of constraints:

  - *Physical* constraints – using the scroll bar for example. The constraints of the shaft restrict movement to up and down (for vertical bars) or left and right (for horizontal bars). You would recognise the constraint and not try to move diagonally.

  - *Semantic* constraints depend on the meaningfulness of the situation and upon the user's knowledge of the world. The recycle bin icon is semantically constrained because it is on the desktop, whereas a bin would normally be under the desk. Provided users understand why such semantic distortions have been introduced, it is not a problem.

  - *Cultural* constraints – like we know which is the gents' and which is the ladies' toilet – because the symbols, although not looking like what they are meant to represent, are still recognisable and understood. If we see a bold outlined exclamation mark we understand that it represents a warning.

  - *Logical* constraints – for example, the order in which items are displayed in menus is logically constrained by appearing as lists. It would not seem logical if items were randomly displayed across the screen.

- *Mappings.* This refers to the layout of objects on the screen – attempting to convey conceptual nearness by means of spatial nearness, for example. Norman[18] uses the layout for cooker rings and controls as an example of bad mapping: in many designs it is not obvious which knob controls which ring – the layout does not convey information by use of spatial clues. In a taxonomy subjects that are close to each other conceptually should be close to each other within the hierarchy.

- *Feedback.* This is exceptionally important – sending back to the user information about what has been done and what the result of their action is. Without the egg timer symbol on the screen we would not know whether or not the system was responding to our input, for example.

Now it is possible to encapsulate the above exploration of concepts in HCI in the form of six essentials of user-centred interface design.

- *Intuitiveness.* It is generally believed that the most fundamental quality of any good user interface should be that it is intuitive. This is something that is very often said about Internet search tools for example. The problem is that what is intuitive to one user may not be intuitive to another user. In any event, a reasonable definition of an intuitive interface is that it is an interface that is easy to learn and one that requires only minimal instruction or training. Icons (back to the use of metaphors again) can help to make an interface intuitive if they are well designed, but as in the example of the Internet Explorer toolbar, text labels can also help. If text labels are used, then they should be concise and unambiguous.

- *Consistency.* It is nice if there is consistency between applications; within an application consistency is absolutely essential. Use of labels and icons must be consistent – the same label or icon must always mean the same thing and represent the same concept. Objects should also be placed in a consistent manner. Most interfaces make use of permanent objects – the Internet Explorer toolbar again. It is good practice to have permanent objects on your screen – they are reference points around which your users can navigate. If your users get lost, then they can find their way back to somewhere familiar – Internet Explorer's Back and Home buttons are a good example of this.

- *Simplicity.* The principle of Occam's razor suggests that the best solution to a problem is the most simple one. An indication of simplicity is the number of keystrokes or mouse clicks required to complete a particular task – the fewer the better. In 1949 Zipf proposed that in any situation people attempt to minimise effort.[19] He was writing about cognitive effort but his 'principle of least effort' can also be applied to physical effort. Zipf's principle basically states that people want to do as little as possible in order to achieve their goals. Simplicity helps: fewer items to scan and extract information from, fewer actions to complete a task. There is often a temptation to make an interface all singing and all dancing. This is usually a mistake, unless tools or features are needed by all your users then they should not all be on the interface.

- *Prevention and forgiveness.* It is better to prevent your users from doing something inappropriate than to let them do it and then show them an error message. You can disable certain functions until conditions are right for them to be performed. Text boxes requiring an OK or a Cancel response to confirm an action are commonplace. Are you sure you want to delete this file? Are you sure you want to quit this application without saving your work? If a user does something inappropriate then allow them to 'undo' it.

- *Aesthetics.* It has already been noted that it is important that the interface looks good. An aesthetically pleasing user interface increases user satisfaction. It is the aesthetics of the interface that form a major part of the focus of the next section.

Display design

Having covered the elements of HCI and interface design in general and theoretical terms, this section will explore more practical issues around layout, navigation, graphics and colour.

It has already been noted that first impressions are extremely important: the attractiveness (or unattractiveness) of the display may determine whether or not people will use a system. No matter how good the quality of the information contained within the system, no matter how good the menu structure is, no matter how powerful the retrieval software, no matter how carefully user models have been incorporated into the system design – if the display does not look good, the result is negative affect and dissatisfied users.

It is worth pointing out again that good display design is dependent on a thorough knowledge of user tasks. Nielsen points out that one of the fundamental errors in design is 'structuring the site to mirror the way the company is structured. Instead the site should be structured to mirror the users' tasks and their views of the information space.'[20] A good display will provide all the data that will take the user through a sequence of tasks – so this is not just about aesthetics. Good display design borrows a lot from the arts and graphic design, but it is also about providing the right information in the right order to cater for user needs, tasks and resources.

Good display design must take account of the six essentials of user-centred design noted previously. Consistency can be achieved by using style sheets: it is good practice to use a single style sheet for all the pages on your site, or possibly a few coordinated ones if you have pages with very different needs – primarily for navigation or primarily for display of content for example.[21] This ensures visual continuity – text and basic layout will look the same throughout the site. To achieve this kind of consistency, it is essential that content creators use style sheets. Nielsen also reminds us that: 'Simplicity should be the goal of page design. Users are rarely on a site to enjoy the design; instead they prefer to focus on the content.'[22] Good design allows users to focus on content; bad design will generally detract from the content by engendering those feelings of hatred and anger mentioned earlier.

The complexity of display design can be illustrated in the work of Smith and Mosier who came up with a list of 162 guidelines, including:

- maintain consistent format from one display to another;
- use affirmative rather than negative statements;
- adopt a logical principle by which to order lists; where no other principle applies, order lists alphabetically;
- left-justify columns of alphabetic data to allow rapid scanning;
- use colour coding for applications in which users must distinguish rapidly among several categories of data.[23]

A lot of the design principles seem to be pretty much based on common sense, but we have all seen enough examples of poor interface and poor display design to know that it is not always straightforward to design something that looks attractive and is easy to use.

A list of 162 guidelines is rather daunting – how can you apply all of those in practice? To simplify somewhat, Mullet and Sano outlined six categories of principles to consider in display design:

- elegance and simplicity;
- scale, contrast and proportion;
- organisation and visual structure;
- module and program;
- image and representation;
- style.[24]

These six principles cover things like effective use of menus and hierarchies, consistency of display, effective use of colour, effective grouping of information items, effective use of different font sizes and, importantly, appropriateness in relation to the tasks supported. In fact they deal with a lot of the issues already considered in this and previous chapters.

Having looked at basic principles, the rest of this chapter will consider four aspects of display design in more depth and with a more practical approach.

Screen layout

Tidwell states that 'Page layout is the art of manipulating the user's attention on a page to convey meaning, sequence, and points of interaction.'[25] Careful composition of the page serves two purposes: to guide the viewer's attention to the main points of interest and to provide aesthetic balance. The aim is to enable the user to extract information quickly and efficiently and achieve an appropriate balance between navigation options and content.

One area of research that is relevant here is that of picture asymmetry: objects in a picture, or on a screen, assume a greater or lesser importance depending on whether they appear on the left or right side. In practice it has been found that the left side of the screen is capable of supporting more weight (density or mass). Objects placed in the right side of the picture assume a greater weight with the result that large masses (for example images or blocks of colour) can unbalance the whole display.[26] Another concept that can influence screen layout is that of the 'golden section' or 'golden ratio'. A long established convention in art is to place the dominant subject in a picture on the golden section. Dividing for ideal proportions tends to produce the ratio of approximately two-thirds to one-third. Jones states that this ratio does seem to work well in practice: 'If the picture is divided into thirds, both horizontally and vertically, the points of intersection are the areas most suitable for the placing of points of interest.'[27] So it is well established that applying the golden ratio can help to draw attention to points of interest. Recent research shows that this does not, however, assist in retrieving information from a web page. Van Schaik[28] has shown that extracting information from a web page with a left-side navigation bar and right-side frame for content takes longer if the page is laid out in accordance with the golden ratio. Ability to extract information quickly was improved when the space given to the navigation bar was reduced.

Whether the navigation bar is on the left or right of the screen does not seem to have any effect. So here we have an apparent conflict between functionality and aesthetics. The best advice would certainly be to design for efficiency of retrieval – a web page can be aesthetically appealing even if it does not conform to the aesthetic convention.

The layout of the page will also depend on its content: a home page, an intermediate navigation page and a content page will probably have different layouts, although all should have permanent objects as navigation aids and all should conform to a chosen style sheet.

The examples shown in Figures 5.7, 5.8 and 5.9 from the British Library website illustrate alternative page layouts very effectively. The home page (Figure 5.7) has the highest visual impact with an emphasis on navigation options and graphics. The page is divided into the banner and global navigation (permanent objects) options at the top, then three main blocks of navigation options: left, centre and right of screen. The intermediate navigation page (Figure 5.8) has a hierarchically organised series of menu choices, but note that the global navigation options (About Us, Collections, Catalogues, Services, What's On, News, Contact Us) are still present. The page devoted to content (Figure 5.9) has a different balance: the banner and global navigation options are again present, but the majority of the screen is devoted to text with a narrower navigation bar on the left of the page.

The BBC's home page is also divided into three main blocks of navigation options and the layout clearly conforms to the golden ratio, with the main browsing menu at the left of the screen taking up one-third of the total area (see Figure 5.10). You will see this basic pattern of dividing the home page into a banner and then two or three blocks of navigation/content in most websites. Subsidiary pages will vary depending on purpose: navigation, content, input.

Nielsen states that:

> As a rule of thumb, content should account for at least half of a page's design, and preferably closer to 80 percent. Navigation should be kept below 20 percent of the space for destination pages, although navigation options may account for much higher proportions of home pages and intermediate navigation pages.[29]

Whether this rule is adhered to will depend on the purpose of the site. If the site carries large blocks of text then the layout of the British Library content page is an effective way to present it. Other sites may devote more screen space to navigation options even at the content level.

Figure 5.7 British Library: home page

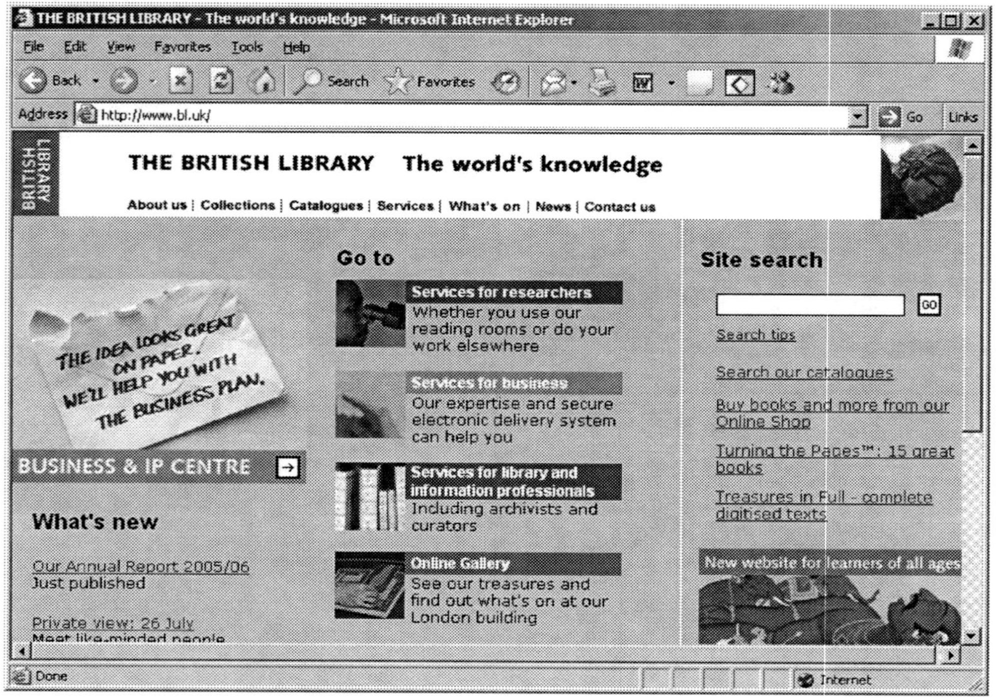

Source: *http://www.bl.uk*

Figure 5.8   British Library: intermediate navigation page (from the site map)

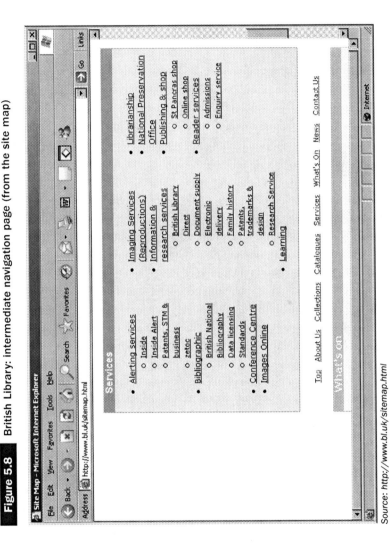

Figure 5.9 British Library: content page

Source: http://www.bl.uk/services/bibliographic/natbib.html

Figure 5.10 bbc.co.uk: home page

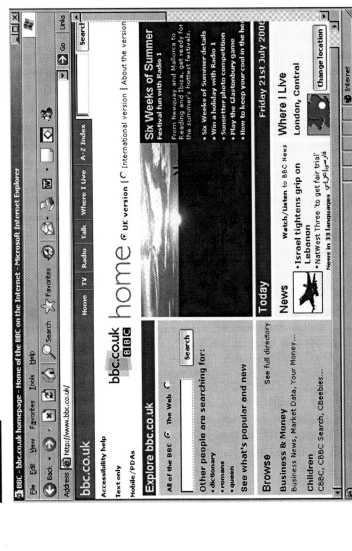

Source: http://www.bbc.co.uk

In the examples from the *Guardian* website in Figures 5.11 and 5.12 we can see that the content page largely mirrors the homepage in that content is restricted to a band in the centre of the screen, with navigation options on the left and a broad band of white space on the right. This helps consistency in that subsidiary pages have the same basic layout as the home page. This actually works quite well in this example as the news stories are quite brief; for longer documents the amount of scrolling down the page to read the text would be problematic.

Navigation

There are three fundamental questions in navigation: Where am I? Where have I been? Where can I go next? In 1986 Jeff Conklin[30] observed that users of hypertexts, then an emerging technology, were in danger of being 'lost in hyperspace'. In navigating an information resource it is all too easy to become disorientated: you are not sure where you are now, where you were and where you should go next. The 'back' button provided by browsers like Internet Explorer is very useful, because it at least helps you to retrace your steps until you get to somewhere you recognise. But, obviously, it is better to have orientation cues on the page so that the user maintains an awareness of their location within the information architecture.

Navigation starts at the home page. Nielsen states that: 'A home page should offer three features: a directory of the site's main content areas, a summary of the most important news or promotions, and a search feature.'[31] We have already seen examples of home pages with these features; they are standard across most well designed websites.

In the examples shown in Figures 5.13 and 5.14, although the websites serve different audiences, the navigation features are almost identical: both sites have a prominent search box, both have a series of clickable menu choices, both have part of the screen space devoted to links to news or features. The Epicurious site is a regular recipient of a Webby award,[32] praised for both good design and good content.

Users navigate a website by typing requests in a search box or by using clickable links. Both on the home page and on subsidiary pages there are three main types of links:

- *Structural navigation links*. These outline the structure of the information space. Examples are home page buttons and links to

Figure 5.11 Guardian.co.uk: home page

Source: http://www.guardian.co.uk

Figure 5.12 Guardian.co.uk: content page

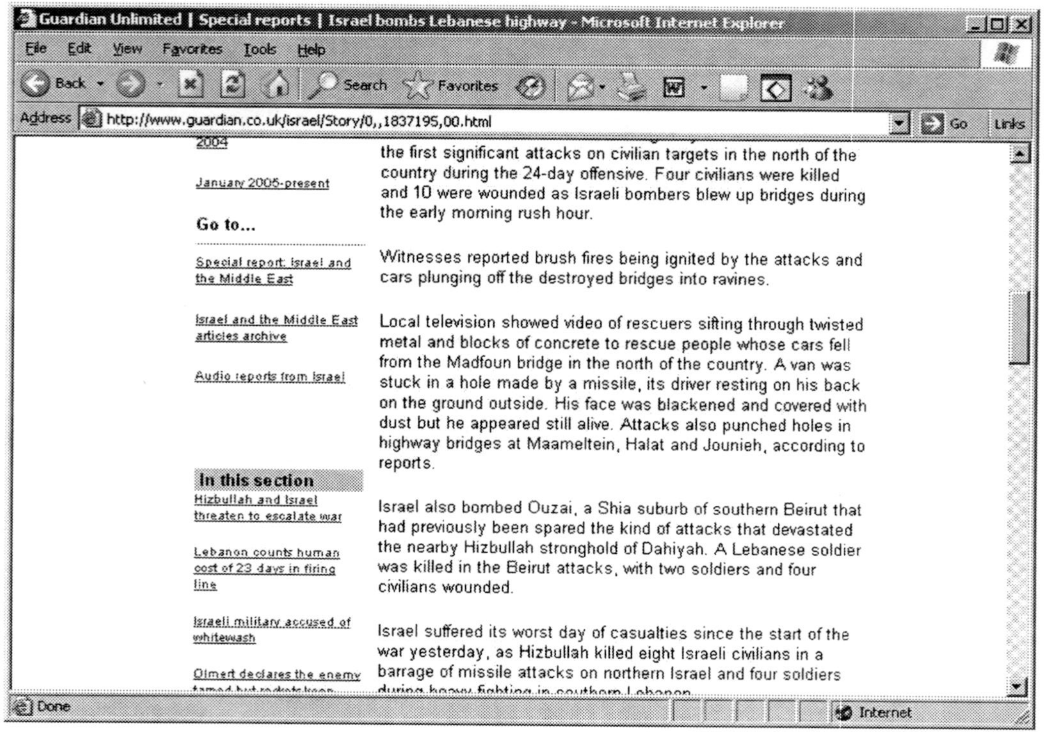

Guardian Unlimited | Special reports | Israel bombs Lebanese highway - Microsoft Internet Explorer

File Edit View Favorites Tools Help

Back ▾ | Search ⭐ Favorites | Go Links

Address 🔗 http://www.guardian.co.uk/israel/Story/0,,1837195,00.html

2004

January 2005-present

Go to...

Special report: Israel and
the Middle East

Israel and the Middle East
articles archive

Audio reports from Israel

In this section

Hizbullah and Israel
threaten to escalate war

Lebanon counts human
cost of 23 days in firing
line

Israeli military accused of
whitewash

Olmert declares the enemy
timed but his dedalare

the first significant attacks on civilian targets in the north of the
country during the 24-day offensive. Four civilians were killed
and 10 were wounded as Israeli bombers blew up bridges during
the early morning rush hour.

Witnesses reported brush fires being ignited by the attacks and
cars plunging off the destroyed bridges into ravines.

Local television showed video of rescuers sifting through twisted
metal and blocks of concrete to rescue people whose cars fell
from the Madfoun bridge in the north of the country. A van was
stuck in a hole made by a missile, its driver resting on his back
on the ground outside. His face was blackened and covered with
dust but he appeared still alive. Attacks also punched holes in
highway bridges at Maameltein, Halat and Jounieh, according to
reports.

Israel also bombed Ouzai, a Shia suburb of southern Beirut that
had previously been spared the kind of attacks that devastated
the nearby Hizbullah stronghold of Dahiyah. A Lebanese soldier
was killed in the Beirut attacks, with two soldiers and four
civilians wounded.

Israel suffered its worst day of casualties since the start of the
war yesterday, as Hizbullah killed eight Israeli civilians in a
barrage of missile attacks on northern Israel and four soldiers
during heavy fighting in southern Lebanon.

Done   Internet

Figure 5.13 TFPL: home page

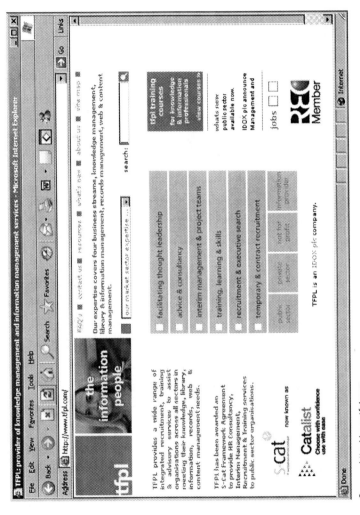

Source: http://www.tfpl.com

Figure 5.14 Epicurious.com: home page

Source: http://www.epicurious.com

subordinate pages. These links are the primary means of allowing users to navigate the website.

■ *Associative links.* These are usually underlined and/or colour highlighted words or phrases within the content of the page. Clicking on an associative link will take the users to pages or other websites with more information about the anchor text. The British Library content page (see Figure 5.9) has several associative links all highlighted in blue. Clicking on any of the highlighted words will take the user straight to the associated text. It is important to be relatively constrained in supplying associative links; only the most important words and phrases should be made into hypertext links. Too much highlighting on the page will interfere with the reading of the text and users may find themselves exploring links that take them to parts of the website that are only of marginal interest. This essentially encourages the 'wandering' behaviour described in Chapter 2.

■ *See also lists of additional references.* These help users to find what they want if the current page does not contain the information they need.[33]

Figure 5.15 from the Open Directory shows 'see also' lists detailing other parts of the directory's hierarchy where users might find information on their topic. Also at the top of the screen are 'breadcrumbs', explained in more detail below, which show the user where they currently are within the directory's hierarchy. A search box is also offered if users cannot locate the needed information by following links.

Whether users type requests in a search box or click on a series of menu choices, various devices can aid them in navigating the information space – helping them to know where they are, where they have been and where they can go next. Navigation can be helped by:

■ *A site map.* A site map is offered by most commercial websites. While potentially useful, site maps are often no more than alphabetically arranged lists of contents and so have limited use as a navigation aid. Certainly this kind of basic site map can help a user to grasp the coverage of the information space, but, unless some form of hierarchical structuring is applied, it will not convey any information about the overall layout of the site. If a user enters the site map from anywhere other than the home page it will not actually provide the contextual information they need to tell them where they are, it will simply allow them to jump to another part of the site. The British Library site map (see Figure 5.7) does apply clustering and display of hierarchy which help users to grasp the overall layout of the site. The

Figure 5.15 Open Directory: navigation links

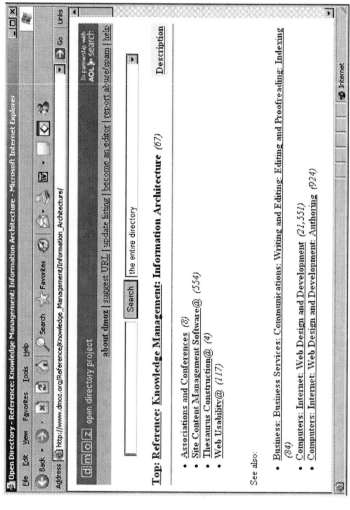

BBC website does not offer a site map per se but has an A–Z index that performs essentially the same function (see Figure 5.16).

- *Permanent objects.* One example is the provision of a global navigation bar. Use of permanent objects has already been mentioned in the context of consistency. Permanent objects are, of course, provided by the user's Internet browser. We have already seen the Internet Explorer toolbar; the Firefox browser toolbar utilises the same basic objects: back, forward, refresh, stop and home (see Figure 5.17). Users can also quickly and easily customise the toolbar to create new permanent objects. The back button is essential – if users become disorientated or jump to a web page that does not contain the needed information, then they can quickly and easily retrace their steps. The favourites or bookmark options are also very useful navigation aids in that users can set up shortcuts to sites or pages they need to access on a regular basis. Permanent objects can also be embedded in websites, usually as a series of clickable links at the top and/or bottom of each page. It is good practice to offer a link to the homepage at the very least.

- *Breadcrumbs.* Essentially this is a 'you are here' device that uses display of hierarchy. We have already seen breadcrumbs in the Open Directory and British Library content page examples in Figures 5.5 and 5.9. The advantage of breadcrumbs over the back or home buttons is that users can jump immediately to an intermediate place in the hierarchy, not simply go one step back or right to the beginning. Nielsen points out that: 'A breadcrumb navigation list has the benefit of being extremely simple and taking up minimum space on the page.'[34]

- *New window.* Instead of jumping to a new page when the user performs an action, a new window is opened. The advantage of using this device is that it is easy to get back to where you were simply by closing the window. The new window can also be resized so that you can compare the anchor text and the window content on the same screen. A problem may arise if the user clicks on links within the new window that open further windows; one new window is useful, several can be confusing.

- *Colour coding of sections.* This provides an instantly recognisable cue. Tidwell says that: 'Colour-coding works to distinguish one section from another, it makes the boundaries clear.'[35] Also, because colour coding distinguishes clusters of similar items, it can help users to create a mental map of the information space; a good map makes it easier to navigate. Colour can, of course, serve to increase the visual

Figure 5.16   BBC: A–Z

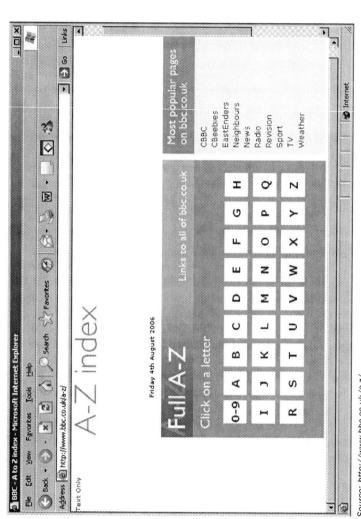

Figure 5.17 Firefox browser

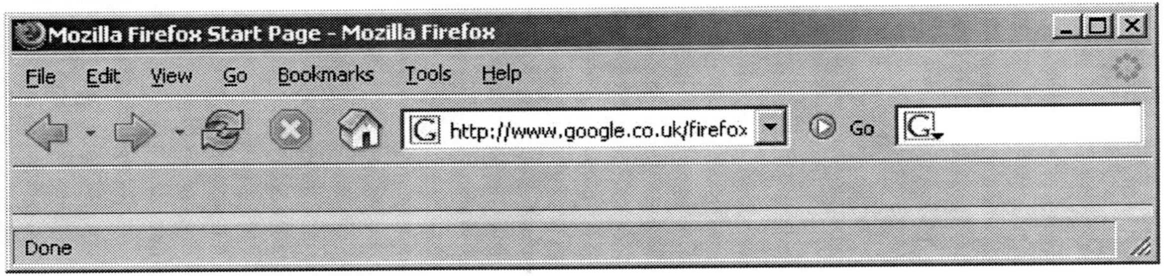

appeal of a site. The British Library site uses colour coding. Each of the main areas of the site is consistently identified by a particular colour: blue for collections, green for services, and so on.

All of the above are simple and effective devices to assist in navigation of the information space. Any well designed website will include a variety of navigation aids as appropriate. It is quite easy to test whether effective navigation tools have been incorporated into the design of a site; if when exploring a site you have to resort to the back button on your browser as the only means of becoming reorientated, then navigation could be improved.

Graphics

Graphics include illustrations, animations, video and fonts. Whether or not graphic devices are used extensively in a website will depend on the purpose of the site. It is appropriate to make a point about novelty here. A lot of websites that receive Webby awards use eye-catching and novel graphics and fonts. This may be good to attract attention, but it will quickly lose its appeal. An intranet is a resource to be used daily: a more classic approach to design and understated use of graphics will have a wider and more lasting appeal.

Two of the most popular search tools on the web have a very different approach to the use of graphics. The Google home page has become a design classic (see Figure 5.18). It has a minimalist look, making attractive use of colour in the banner, but otherwise utilising white space and blue text. The purpose of the site is immediately apparent, with the search box prominently placed in the middle of the screen. Users are not distracted by animations or advertising.

The uk.yahoo.com home page again uses blue text but that is the only similarity to Google. The Yahoo home page has minimal white space – the screen is filled with menus and links to advertising (see Figure 5.19). This is not necessarily a negative point. Yahoo serves as a portal as well as a search engine. It appeals to a different type of user: one who wants to have one-click access to a range of services and sites as well as being able to search the web.

It has previously been noted that an organisation will probably have two interfaces: one for external users and one for internal users. For a professional look and feel, use of illustrations should be restricted on the external user interface and should probably be omitted altogether on the

Figure 5.18 Google: home page

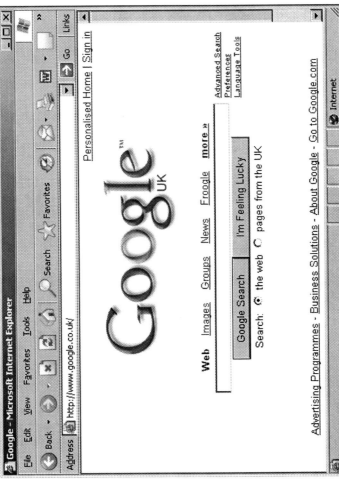

Source: http://www.google.co.uk

Figure 5.19 Yahoo: home page

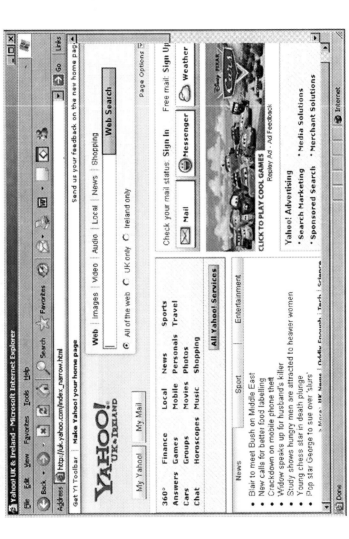

Source: *http://uk.yahoo.com/index_narrow.html*

interface to the intranet. Illustrations can enhance the aesthetic appeal of a website, but overuse of graphic devices can make a screen look cluttered and will result in longer download times.

As can be seen in the examples in Figures 5.20 and 5.21, the extranet and intranet home pages have an entirely different look and feel. Consistency is achieved through use of colour and the university logo. Obviously the intranet homepage would not appeal to external users wanting to find out more about the university – it is poor in terms of visual impact and would not attract and hold a user's attention. The aim of the intranet is not to attract attention but to provide quick links to applications and resources for frequent users. The basic message for designers is that illustrations must be used with care.

Selection of fonts to use in a website can help to create an organisational identity as well as assisting users to extract information by enhancing readability. Garrett points out that some fonts are difficult to read on a website because of the limited resolution of computer screens.[36] Legibility certainly is a primary concern when selecting fonts. An obvious but important point to make is that font size affects legibility. Although internal users will probably be using standard workstations on which legibility testing has been performed as part of the overall design process, external users may have screens that make smaller font sizes difficult to read. It is also good practice to limit the number of fonts used across a site; this aids consistency, helps to establish identity and promotes a sense of cohesion. Tidwell suggests that only one font should be used for content, but that it is appropriate to use other fonts to highlight navigation options and headings.[37]

Colour

Effective use of colour can greatly enhance the attractiveness of the display and can certainly increase user satisfaction. On the other hand, poor use of colour can have a powerful negative effect, and we have all come across websites where the use of colour has put us off immediately – the importance of first impressions again. This is certainly not a straightforward issue. What appeals to some users will not appeal to others – that is why some commercial applications allow you to customise the colour scheme. To a great extent, perceived attractiveness depends upon individual colour preferences, and so there is no simple set of rules about use of colour. However, Shneiderman,[38] among others, provides a

Figure 5.20 London Metropolitan University: extranet home page

Source: http://www.londonmet.ac.uk

Figure 5.21 London Metropolitan University: intranet home page

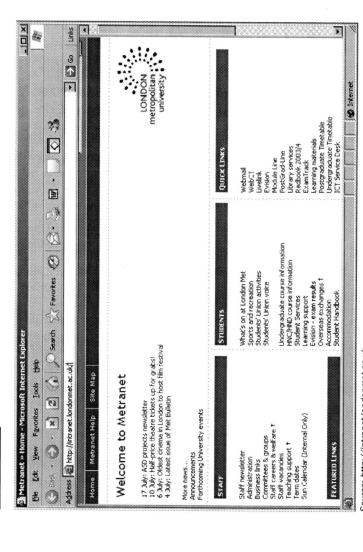

Source: *http://intranet.londonmet.ac.uk*

set of guidelines, including the benefits and dangers, for designers that will form the framework of an exploration of the use of colour in web design.

- *Use colour conservatively.* Limit the number of colours used in the display. Often a colourful display looks quite effective when you first enter a site but then when you try to actually read what is on the screen problems become apparent; it is difficult to extract content. Overuse of colour can also lead users into looking for relationships that do not exist. It is often suggested to limit the number of colours on a single screen to four, with a maximum of seven over the whole series of displays.

- *Utilise colour to speed task completion.* We have already seen that careful use of colour coding can indicate relationships between items on the screen for example. Misuse of colour can make text difficult to read: bear in mind that some colour combinations do not work well. Maximum legibility is achieved by high contrast: light on dark or dark on light. Plain colour backgrounds rather than patterned backgrounds also aid legibility.

- *Ensure that colour coding supports the task.* We have already seen that colour coding can aid navigation by creating easily identifiable clusters of related items. In an information retrieval system, for example, highlighting key terms within retrieved documents should allow the user to assess their relevance quickly.

- *Use colour changes to indicate status changes.* An example is to change the colour of menu items that have been clicked on so that the user can immediately identify whether or not they have already explored a link. This is standard across most websites and is useful in avoiding duplication of effort.

- *Allow some degree of user control.* As noted previously, the way people respond to colour is largely a matter of personal preference. The interface of the Hotbot[39] search engine is rather restrained now, but in the past it had much more extensive use of vivid green and red in its screen design. As some users hated the colours they welcomed the ability to select an alternative 'skin'. It may be appropriate to allow users to switch the colour coding off. For example, if the user has retrieved a full-text document, it may be easier to read if the key terms are not highlighted throughout.

- *Design for monochrome first.* Do not just rely on colour to identify headings or groups of related items – use different font sizes and effective use of spacing as well. The layout of information on the screen is important and it is often more effective to design the layout before adding colour.

- *Consider the needs of visually impaired users.* There are guidelines for this – useful sources of information are the W3C[40] and RNIB[41] websites. A very simple point to remember is that red-green colour-blindness is the most common form.

- *Use colour to help in formatting.* So, for example, make titles stand out by using a different colour to the main text. Again colour coding can be used to group related items.

- *Be consistent in colour coding.* Use the same colour coding rules throughout the system. Using the British Library example noted previously, if 'services' are represented by the colour green, then only use that colour for services. If error messages appear in red, then make sure all error messages appear in red.

- *Be aware of expectations about colour codes.* These are to some extent culturally determined, but we commonly understand red to mean danger, yellow for warning, green for go. Different users may understand different sets of conventions.

- *Use colour in graphic displays for greater information density.* This is especially good for presenting information in graphs and charts.

Effective use of colour in a display can have a powerful positive impact. Equally, poor or overuse of colour can provoke a negative emotional response which will affect use of the system. It is essential to design with all users in mind, including visually impaired users who may find it difficult to extract information from a screen that uses colour injudiciously. It should be noted that some colour pairings may cause problems for all users. For example, too much red and blue on the same display can be problematic and can cause physical discomfort – that is not about aesthetics, it is about physiology. To see the effect of different colours in a screen display it is useful to look at some of the sites offering free templates for web designers, for example Open Source Web Design.[42] The basic page layout may be identical across many of the templates, but use of different colours creates a very different feel. Tidwell[43] also includes a series of examples that show how identical content is affected by different page layout and use of colour. It is becoming more difficult to find examples of really poor use of colour in websites. Everyone tends to copy everyone else and you find a lot of use of muted colours with the emphasis on the blue palette. This may not be to everyone's taste and is perhaps rather boring.

Summary

This chapter has served to introduce the principles of interface and display design. We have seen how a range of interrelated concepts impact on the visual appeal and usability of a web-based information system. Coverage here has been necessarily brief, but the look and feel of the information resource is an integral part of the information architecture as a whole. Recommendations for further reading are provided at the end of the chapter for anyone wanting to explore HCI and interface design in more depth.

The Webby Awards have been referred to previously. To summarise the main principles of interface and display design it is useful to frame a discussion around the Webby Awards' six judging criteria[44] as these encapsulate all the issues examined above.

- *Content.* This is the first criterion cited and emphasises the point that, no matter how beautifully designed the information space is, if the content does not support user needs and tasks, then the system is not achieving its purpose. Content can be in any format: text, graphics, video and so on; form is unimportant. Quality and fitness for purpose are the key issues.

- *Structure and navigation.* This refers to layout, organisation and linking of content. We have examined screen or page layout and navigation features and links: devices that tell the user where they are, where they have been and where they can go next. Consistency of screen layout, provision of permanent objects and visual cues like colour coding can help the user to develop an appropriate mental model of the information space.

- *Visual design.* This is vitally important in promoting positive affect. The visual design of an information space can have an emotional impact on users. If the emotion inspired is hatred, then the system either will not be used at all or will be used only grudgingly. We have also seen that aesthetic principles applied to screen layout and use of graphics and colour can speed or slow completion of tasks and extraction of information.

- *Functionality.* The site should use appropriate technology and work efficiently. Overuse of graphics, for example, can affect functionality if pages are slow to load. If part of the system is intended for external use, then design should take account of external users who may have different hardware configurations and access to different software.

We have seen how choice of font and font size may affect legibility and therefore functionality. Simple devices like the provision of files in alternative formats like HTML and PDF can aid functionality. The needs of users with visual impairment or other disabilities should also be taken into account.

- *Interactivity*. The web is designed for interactivity not passivity. An information resource should promote information and knowledge sharing and it can do this by providing various fora for interactive communication. As well as providing access to documentation, the information architecture has to support information flow across the organisation by providing access to e-mail, e-bulletin boards, news and events information and so on. All these interactive elements have to be part of the overall design.

- *Overall experience*. This includes all of the above. Here we are also concerned with emotional response again and with individual satisfaction ratings. Do users feel positively about the system? There are many measures of system effectiveness which we will explore in the final chapter, but arguably the most important – and the most difficult to define – is whether or not users like the system. Good design certainly helps to increase satisfaction levels.

Finally, individual organisations should draw up a set of formal guidelines for display design – tailored to local needs. It is certainly useful to have some kind of house style. Also, make sure you consult with the users of the system and do thorough testing and evaluation before full implementation. When designing, or indeed evaluating, the interface, always keep in mind the basic principles of consistency, simplicity, prevention and forgiveness, and aesthetics. Make sure that the design and layout supports user tasks, that suitable navigation options are provided and that appropriate use is made of graphics and colour.

Further reading

There are many very good basic introductions to the principles of interface and display design. Jakob Nielsen has written extensively on the topic and his book listed below is a readable introduction to many of the concepts covered in this chapter:

- Nielsen, J. (2000) *Designing Web Usability: The Practice of Simplicity*. Indianapolis, IN: New Riders.

Jenifer Tidwell's book is also recommended:

- Tidwell, J. (2006) *Designing Interfaces.* Sebastopol, CA: O'Reilly.

For entertaining and erudite treatment of design principles generally, two books by Donald Norman are highly recommended:

- Norman, D.A. (2002) *The Design of Everyday Things.* New York: Basic Books.

- Norman, D.A. (2004) *Emotional Design: Why We Love (or Hate) Everyday Things.* New York: Basic Books.

It is worth exploring some of the websites cited above. The Webbys site at *http://www.webbyawards.com* certainly merits a closer look. As well as details of the criteria used in evaluating websites, it provides links to all the nominated sites and award winners, so is an excellent starting point for anyone wishing to see examples of well designed websites.

References

1. Preece, J. et al. (1994) *Human-Computer Interaction.* Wokingham: Addison-Wesley, p. 5.
2. Norman, D.A. (2004) *Emotional Design: Why We Love (or Hate) Everyday Things.* New York: Basic Books, p. 7.
3. Shneiderman, B. (2003) *Leonardo's Laptop: Human Needs and the New Computing Technologies.* Cambridge, MA: MIT Press, p. 14.
4. Kuhlthau, C.C. (1994) *Seeking Meaning: A Process Approach to Library and Information Services.* Norwood, NJ: Ablex, p. 28.
5. Tidwell, J. (2006) *Designing Interfaces.* Sebastopol, CA: O'Reilly, p. 269.
6. *http://credibility.stanford.edu/* (accessed 27 July 2006).
7. Nielsen, J. (2000) *Designing Web Usability: The Practice of Simplicity.* Indianapolis, IN: New Riders, p. 274.
8. ACM SIGCHI (1992) *Curriculum for Human-Computer Interaction.* New York: ACM Specialist Interest Group on Computer-Human Interaction Curriculum Development Group, p. 6.
9. Human-Computer Interaction (2006) *http://en.wikipedia.org/wiki/Human-computer_interaction* (accessed 19 July 2006).
10. Booth, P.A. (1989) *An Introduction to Human-Computer Interaction.* Hove: Erlbaum, p. 7.

11. Norman, D.A. and Draper, S.W (1986) *User-Centered System Design: New Perspectives on Human-Computer Interaction.* Hillsdale, NJ: Erlbaum, p. 46.
12. Lidwell, W. et al. (2003) *Universal Principles of Design.* Gloucester, MA: Rockport, p. 130.
13. Lakoff, G. and Johnson, M. (1981) *Metaphors We Live By.* Chicago: University of Chicago Press, p. 5.
14. Hutchins, E. et al (1986) 'Direct manipulation interfaces', in D.A. Norman and S.W. Draper (eds), *User-Centered System Design: New Perspectives on Human-Computer Interaction.* Hillsdale, NJ: Erlbaum.
15. Norman, D.A. (1988) *The Design of Everyday Things.* New York: Basic Books.
16. Darnell, M.J. (2006) *Bad Human Factors Designs, http://www .baddesigns.com/* (accessed 19 July 2006).
17. Norman, op. cit., pp. 82–99.
18. Ibid., p. 75.
19. Zipf, G.K. (1949) *Human Behaviour and the Principle of Least Effort.* Wokingham: Addison-Wesley.
20. Nielsen, op. cit., p. 15.
21. Ibid., p. 81.
22. Ibid., p. 97.
23. Smith, S.L. and Mosier, J.N. (1986) *Guidelines for Designing User Interface Software, http://hcibib.org/sam/* (accessed 19 July 2006).
24. Mullet, K. and Sano, D. (1995) *Designing Visual Interfaces.* Englewood Cliffs, NJ: Sunsoft Press.
25. Tidwell, op. cit., p. 89.
26. Millerson, G. (1968) *The Technique of Television Production*, 7th edn. Woburn, MA: Focal Press.
27. Jones, P. (1969) *The Technique of the Television Cameraman*, 2nd edn. Woburn, MA: Focal Press, p. 81.
28. Van Schaik, P. and Ling, J. (2006) 'The effects of graphical display and screen ratio on information retrieval in web pages', *Computers in Human Behavior*, 22 (5): 870–84.
29. Nielsen, op. cit., p. 22.
30. Conklin, J. (1987) 'Hypertext: an introduction and survey', *IEEE Computer*, September, pp. 17–41.
31. Nielsen, op. cit., p. 168.
32. Webby Awards, *http://www.webbyawards.com* (accessed 31 July 2006).
33. Nielsen, op. cit., p. 5.
34. Ibid., p. 206.

35. Tidwell, op. cit., p. 82.
36. Garrett, J.J. (2003) *The Elements of User Experience: User-Centered Design for the Web*. Indianapolis, IN: New Riders, p. 155.
37. Tidwell, op. cit., p. 287.
38. Shneiderman, B. (2004) *Designing the User Interface: Strategies for Effective Human-Computer Interaction*, 4th edn. Boston: Addison-Wesley.
39. Hotbot: *http://www.hotbot.com* (accessed 1 August 2006).
40. W3C (1999) *Web Content Accessibility Guidelines 1.0*, *http://www.w3.org/ TR/WAI-WEBCONTENT/* (accessed 19 July 2006).
41. RNIB (2006) *See It Right Guidelines*, *http://www.rnib.org .uk/xpedio/groups/public/documents/PublicWebsite/public_ seeitright.hcsp* (accessed 19 July 2006).
42. Open Source Web Design: *http://www.oswd.org/* (accessed 1 August 2006).
43. Tidwell, op. cit., pp. 272–8.
44. Webby Awards judging criteria: *http://www.webbyawards.com/ webbys/criteria.php* (accessed 2 August 2006).

Management and maintenance

So far we have concentrated on practical issues around the design of the information architecture. In this penultimate chapter the focus is on management issues. Content management is examined in some depth with a focus on policy and strategy formation. This is followed by a discussion of general roles and responsibilities in maintaining the information architecture. Although this chapter is briefer than the previous chapters, this does not imply that the management and maintenance of the system are less important than the design issues explored elsewhere. A lot of work goes into designing a system that meets the needs of the organisation and the users, but the work does not end when the system is deployed. If the information architecture is to continue to meet organisational and user needs then it must be effectively managed and maintained. Areas explored in this chapter are of concern at the very start of the design process and continue post-implementation.

Content management

Content was mentioned only in passing in the definitions of information architecture cited in Chapter 1, but as we have seen it is not just the structure and the external appearance of the resource that is important: the information itself is of central concern. We looked at content analysis and metadata in Chapter 4 – here we broaden our scope to consider content management. As pointed out previously, no matter how well designed and aesthetically pleasing your system is, no matter how good the architecture is, the system is only going to be of benefit if it includes all the documentation and information its users need, and that presupposes that the information and documentation is effectively managed.

Content analysis and content mapping were previously examined as part of the information architecture development process. They will influence basic functionality, i.e. the range of software applications utilised, and taxonomy creation. Continuing usability of the system depends upon having strategies in place for managing the content. Boiko[1] defines content management as:

> The process behind matching what 'you' have with what 'they' want. 'You' are an organisation with information and functionality of value. 'They' are a set of definable audiences who want that value. Content management is an overall process for collecting, managing and publishing content to any outlet.

The purpose of content management is to control the information life cycle: through creation, approval, updating and weeding. This includes managing documents and managing records – those content components or chunks of information that may be reused or repurposed across the system. It is important to point out that the focus in this section is on managing content, not on content management systems (CMS). There are, of course, commercial CMS that provide software solutions for automatic capture and deployment of content, but decisions have to be made about which CMS will best suit an organisation's needs and, once implemented, the CMS has to be managed. Here the focus is upon strategy and process rather than individual applications.

McKeever[2] outlines a four-layer hierarchy to provide a context for content management which rather neatly demonstrates that content management underpins the whole system architecture (see Figure 6.1). At the top of McKeever's hierarchy is the audience layer: the users of the system, who could be staff and/or customers of the organisation for example. One level below that is the outlet layer: the interface to the system. Below that is the activity layer: where contents are created and deployed, deployment being controlled by content analysis and metadata

Figure 6.1 McKeever's hierarchy

Audience
Outlet
Activity
Content

tagging. At the lowest level is the content itself: the records and documentation that are created, analysed and deployed.

In McKeever's four-layer hierarchy we can see the entire range of information architecture. Information audit and needs analysis examines the audience layer: identifying different types of user and their associated needs. Principles of user-centred design are addressed at the outlet layer, which will support a range of tasks and individual resources. At the activity layer, documents and records are created, categorised and tagged so that they can be represented at the outlet layer and retrieved by the audience. At the content layer is the information itself. Content management incorporates everything from information creation through to its use so does not restrict its sphere of interest to one level. Studying content management requires an examination of the whole system architecture.

Before going on to consider content management strategy, it is useful to look at the process in more detail. Here the focus is on the activity level of McKeever's model and the information life cycle. Several writers including Boiko[3] and Tredinnick[4] map out the information life cycle. Sequential models of the information life cycle are common (see Figure 6.2) but the reality is rather more complex than this would suggest: phases and activities within the information life cycle are iterative.

The first phase is information creation and collection. At lot of people within the organisation may be concerned with this. Staff throughout the organisation may be authors of documents or creators of content. Some people (librarians or information managers for example) may also have responsibility for collecting and making available external documentation or sources of information.

The second phase, which some organisations may ignore, depending on how closely content is managed, is approval. Some organisations will take a laissez-faire approach and allow content creators to decide what should and what should not be accessible. Other organisations will impose some form of centralised control to manage content. Approval may be the responsibility of departmental managers, or it may be the responsibility of an information manager or information management team. Certainly once a document has been created, it has to be approved quickly, so that it can move on to the next phase.

The third phase is deployment or publishing of content. This involves making the content accessible: creating web pages, assigning documentation to a category in a taxonomy, providing metadata to assist retrieval and reuse of information across multiple web pages, and so on. Creators of documents may have responsibility for publishing their own

Figure 6.2 Information life cycle

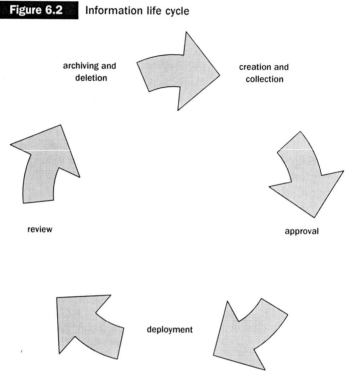

content or the process may be overseen by specialist staff – information managers for example.

The fourth phase is review of content. Once information is published, it is certainly not the end of the life cycle. Content has to be continually reviewed to assess its status: currency, authority, value and so on. The metadata assigned to a document can include information about review: when a document should be updated, when the information it contains will be out of date, when it should have been superseded by a new document. Including review information in the metadata should at least ensure that individual documents are checked for currency and accuracy every month, every three months or whatever period seems to be appropriate. No organisation wants documentation present in their information systems after it has lost its value or relevancy.

The fifth phase is archiving and deletion of content. The review phase will identify documentation that is no longer needed. Some of the information contained in the documents will have been of transient value and the document should therefore be deleted. Other information, while no longer needed, may still have some value to the organisation and should be archived. When organisations relied on paper documentation, archiving was a given. Documents were filed away – in the records management department, in the library, in people's filing cabinets. It is easy to delete digital information, and there has to be a policy drawn up and a strategy implemented whereby important documentation is archived for future reference.

Content management strategy

A content management strategy should address a number of issues that are central to designing, maintaining and managing the information architecture. The strategy should establish roles and responsibilities, improve communication and ensure coordination of all information-related activities. Essentially the strategy should set out a series of objectives for managing content across the organisation, the overall aim being to improve information and resource sharing. It is important that the strategy include all stakeholders: managers, specialists and users. One of the barriers to effective information sharing in organisations is the organisational culture: whether it is exclusive or inclusive, whether it encourages people to be protective of their knowledge or rewards them for sharing it. People will only participate in information and knowledge sharing if they see personal benefits in doing so. It can be very difficult to balance the needs of users and authors with the goals of the organisation, but an inclusive content management strategy can help.

It is useful to divide implementation of the content management strategy into three stages: formulation of policy, planning and deployment. The content management policy would necessarily reflect the overall goals of the organisation. The content management strategy should set out a series of objectives; the policy should provide the means by which the achievement of these objectives can be measured. The UK's e-government policy[5] stresses the setting of goals to help in determining the extent to which the overall strategy is followed and how far the policy guidelines are being met. Brys's paper[6] provides a useful, practical outline of how to implement a content management strategy. Her implementation plan has seven main points, and has been used in the following overview of the various issues.

Formulation of policy

- Emphasise the importance of information and its communication. This can be helped by drawing up clear policies and guidelines.

- Set out clear responsibilities. This should cover all levels: organisational, departmental and individual.

Content management policy would incorporate all aspects of the strategy outlined below, but central to the policy is an emphasis upon the importance of information and its communication within the organisation, and establishment of roles and responsibilities. The policy should clearly state how the content management strategy supports the work of the organisation. It should also set out guidelines about ownership of information and adherence to legal requirements generally. The policy can be quite specific, including things like using the Dublin Core Metadata Element Set to ensure consistency in describing documents. The policy should also specify individual and group responsibilities. For example, authors may be responsible for providing metadata; departmental information managers may be responsible for quality checks and approving publication of documentation.

Planning

- Provide training. For managers, authors and users.

- Communicate clearly and inclusively. By making sure that effective communication channels about the information system are established – possibly through managers at departmental level.

- Emphasise the importance of the information architecture team in providing support and quality control.

The planning phase would emphasise Brys's next three points, which would also be carried through into the deployment phase. Training programmes must be designed prior to implementation. All the training resources must be in place: training staff, accommodation for training workshops and seminars, documentation, a help desk and other online support. Everyone within the organisation should be informed about any changes. It is important in managing change that everyone who will be affected by the change feels that they are stakeholders and that proper consultation has taken place. Their participation in the information audit should help people to feel that their needs are being taken into account. A commonly cited reason for information architecture development is to improve information flow. This suggests that current channels of communication are not very effective which can obviously create problems. A mix of paper, electronic and face-to-face communication may need to be utilised and feedback encouraged. The final point in the planning stage presupposes that there is an information architecture team. If an organisation is willing to invest in improving access to information, then there should be a team of specialists coordinating design, planning and implementation of the new system. If the information architecture team has been involved in the information audit, they should already have quite a high profile within the organisation.

Deployment

- Set out workflow procedures for publication of content.
- Establish best practices. This might be done on a departmental level if general organisational guidelines do not address specific needs.

At the deployment stage, the architecture is in place and the focus is upon its maintenance and effectiveness as an information resource. This involves issues previously outlined – training, for example, will be ongoing – but publication of content and quality issues merit discussion at this stage. Workflow procedures for publication of content should be established to ensure smooth transition through the information life cycle: from creation and collection, through approval, publication, review and disposal. Everyone involved in the process should know exactly what their role is and should perform that role efficiently. Ensuring that information is published quickly is vital, as is ensuring that only current information is on the system. To safeguard the quality of the resource and the information it contains Brys suggests that individual departments or services should establish best practices (and also guidelines where organisational guidelines do not seem to apply). The important point is to ensure that authors' needs are balanced with departmental or service needs and the needs of the organisation as a whole. The need for consistency predicates that certain important decisions should not be left up to individual authors. By delegating responsibility to departments or services, diversity can be accommodated while ensuring a degree of consistency.

This exploration of content management strategy ends with deployment which may suggest completion, but, of course, it does not actually stop there. In a sense, deployment is only the beginning: the architecture is in place, roles and responsibilities have been allocated, now the focus moves from project management to ongoing management and maintenance of the information architecture and its information content.

Management and maintenance issues

There are various questions that any organisation involved in developing an information architecture and implementing a content management system should have considered and found answers to. The same questions should be asked in any organisational context, but there are no definitive answers to them. Solutions will depend upon the needs of the individual organisation.

Who should be responsible for strategy and policy formulation? The final decisions will be made by senior management, but it is important to involve information and technical specialists and, where possible, users. This relates to effective change management. It also relates to an issue raised earlier. It was stated in Chapter 4 on documents and document description that much of the literature on information architecture examines high-level content: subjects that should be present within a taxonomy and organisational needs as revealed in the information audit. That was a top-down approach to system content representing an ideal. Strategy and policy formation is also almost certainly going to represent an ideal – and in one sense that is perfectly acceptable. The strategy, in particular, will reflect the overall goals of the organisation. But by involving people at all levels of the organisation, it should be possible to learn about and incorporate (at least in the policy) what is realistically achievable.

Who should be responsible for design and implementation? It is to be hoped that there will be an information architecture team. Designated, specialist staff should be recruited at the start of the process to provide input into the strategy and policy formation phase, which will feed into the design and of course the implementation. Members of the team should be involved in the information audit. Apart from the need to feed the resulting data into the system design, it will also ensure that eventual users of the system get to know the team. Ultimately, potentially everyone within the organisation will be involved. Users will influence the design and will be involved in testing prototype systems.

Who should be responsible for maintenance of the system? Ideally the information architecture team or an information manager should have overarching responsibility for managing the content of the system as a whole and, of course, the taxonomy. If everyone can add what they like where they like, then a nicely structured search and retrieval tool will quickly descend into chaos.

Who should be responsible for deciding what is included? One of the key issues in records management is deciding what deserves the status of a record. Determining a record's role and function requires objective evaluation and authors might not be the best people to assess whether their documents have a function that merits their publication. If departmental managers are involved in the approval process, then ultimate responsibility will lie with them, but perhaps their focus is rather too narrow. Again, ideally an information manager, or information management team, with an overview of the whole organisation and its needs and the needs of individual members of staff, should be responsible for deciding what resources are included. Another approach is to consider whether everything should be included. If the answer is yes, then that dispenses with the need for someone to make decisions about what is included. But organisations generate enormous amounts of documentation – should everything be accessible to everyone? Also, what is stored and capable of being retrieved within the information system will not necessarily be made available within the taxonomy. Taxonomies should be a means of improving resource sharing. If they grow too large or too complex or if they contain a lot of documentation that is of no possible interest to the majority of users, then they lose their efficiency as information retrieval tools.

Who should be responsible for document description and metadata creation? Someone needs to take responsibility for how the resources are indexed – checking subject metadata and deciding which categories in a taxonomy resources should be allocated to. It seems sensible to leave the metadata creation and categorisation to the originators of documents, but authors cannot be expected to be consistent – although providing a list of descriptors in a glossary or thesaurus can help. It may be safer to leave the subject indexing at least to the information manager or the information team but the volume of work involved may seem to be prohibitive. This has real staffing implications which must be thought through before the system is deployed. In the library environment, cataloguing is no longer seen as a core specialism because the development of cataloguing standards in the MARC formats allowed individual libraries to make use of repositories of bibliographic data. The same is not the case in an organisation, where much of the documentation is unique to that organisation. This means that someone has to do the cataloguing and ideally that person should be a specialist. A recurring theme has been that in order to increase the efficiency of search and retrieval, consistency is vital in describing and categorising documents. Consistency may be dependent upon having a team of people working full-time on metadata checking and creation. This will add another level of quality control; it may also delay publication of content.

Who gets access – does everyone get access to everything? Some information will almost certainly have to be password protected. This also impacts on the taxonomy. Should there be a single taxonomy for the whole organisation or is it more appropriate to have a shared taxonomy plus a series of specialist taxonomies? This seems to be contrary to the whole idea of a taxonomy as a tool to facilitate resource sharing, but some parts of the organisation may be sufficiently specialised to merit their own smaller, highly specialised taxonomies to facilitate resource sharing among a few highly specialised individuals. Some resources might only be for the eyes of certain people within the organisation, so parts of the taxonomy (personnel records and payroll, for example) may have to be closed to groups of users. The taxonomy will be mounted on the organisation's intranet, but is it appropriate to mount parts of it on the extranet? The answer is almost certainly yes. Remember that information chunks can be reused and so will be included in documentation or web pages designed for external users. This introduces a set of new issues around public access and security.

Who should be responsible for deciding what should be removed? Does an information manager decide, or should the creators and/or approvers of documents decide? It seems logical that whoever decides what goes in should be responsible for what comes out. Making decisions about deletion or weeding of content may be straightforward if, for example, an interim report is being superseded by a final report, but the information manager may lack sufficient specialist knowledge to decide when a document contains out-of-date and possibly misleading information, so perhaps authors or other specialist staff must be involved in the weeding process. Metatags can be used to determine the life of a document or to signal when content should be reviewed. But is it appropriate to let authors decide what should be deleted and what should be archived?

All these questions impact on information architecture and content management strategy and all focus primarily on the content itself. Information architecture, in focusing upon structure and design, takes a top-down approach to system development: providing a framework and techniques that assist in the development of ideal information environments. In reality, the architecture is only as good as the information it houses. By focusing on content, the above discussion has outlined a series of management issues that should be addressed to ensure that the reality matches the vision.

Further reading

A good, concise overview of management and maintenance issues in the context of intranets is provided by:

- Tredinnick, L. (2005) *Why Intranets Fail (and How to Fix Them)*. Oxford: Chandos.

References

1. Boiko, B. (2001) 'Understanding content management', *ASIS*, 28, October–November: 8–13.
2. McKeever, S. (2003) 'Understanding Web content management systems', *Industrial Management and Data Systems*, 103 (9): 686–92.
3. Boiko, op. cit.
4. Tredinnick, L. (2005) *Why Intranets Fail (and How to Fix Them)*. Oxford: Chandos.
5. e-Government Policy Framework for Electronic Records Management (2001) available at: *http://www.nationalarchives.gov.uk/ electronicrecords/pdf/egov_ framework.pdf* (accessed 20 August 2006).
6. Brys, C.M. (2004) *Discussion Paper on Content Management Strategy*, University of Glasgow Web Advisory Group, available at: *http://www.gla.ac.uk/infostrat/WAG/paper_cmstrategy.pdf* (accessed 20 August 2006).

Evaluation

This final chapter concentrates on how to evaluate the information architecture and represents an opportunity to provide an overview of the issues covered in this book. Many of the areas covered in previous chapters require the use of some form of evaluation to assess quality and functionality. Evaluation should begin at the start of the design process and continue post-deployment, from evaluation of software applications, interface designs and use of the system and its content.

A dictionary definition of 'evaluate' is simply 'to determine the value of'. This is highly appropriate given that organisations will develop information architecture to add value to their operations. The definition is perhaps rather narrow, however. Evaluation should also be concerned with determining the quality of something. So evaluation, in the context of information architecture, is about judging its value and quality. In terms of the usability of a system evaluation is concerned with assessing effectiveness, efficiency and level of user satisfaction.

The purpose of evaluation research is to assess the effects and/or the effectiveness of something. But it goes beyond simple assessment, by incorporating, as its name implies, value judgements. Evaluation research as we understand it today really originated in the 1960s in the USA where evaluation of large-scale projects was commissioned by the government. These studies often showed that these projects were not achieving the desired results, and the outcome of the evaluation was change. So, to differentiate between evaluation research and research per se, an evaluation is a study with a distinct and often very narrowly defined purpose; it is not exploring something new or different. Evaluation research is usually commissioned by a client or sponsor who dictates both the topic and the scope of the evaluation.

In evaluation research it is important to have an awareness of existing beliefs and expectations. Political influences are often inescapable: the evaluation approach selected, including the evaluation criteria used, may reflect the perspective of one interested party as opposed to another. The sponsor of the research may simply want to use the evaluation to justify choices already made, but evaluation often recommends ways of improving the project evaluated: it is associated with change. As in anything that results in change, clear communication with all stakeholders, not just the sponsor of the evaluation, must be established to ensure recommendations are appropriate and that they are acted upon.

There are several approaches to evaluation research reflecting a range of interpretations and perspectives. These include:

- goal-oriented evaluation;
- user-oriented evaluation;
- experimental evaluation;
- responsive evaluation.

Goal-oriented evaluation uses project-specific goals or objectives as criteria for assessing value. In the context of information architecture this assumes that evaluation has been factored into the strategy formation phase to assist in devising a series of goals and objectives that can be measured. It was noted in the previous chapter that the UK's e-government policy stresses the setting of goals to help in determining the extent to which the overall strategy is being followed and how far the policy guidelines are being met. There is an inherent problem with this type of evaluation: its worth depends upon the appropriateness of the original goals. There can be a temptation to reformulate goals when the outcome of a project is known.

User-oriented evaluation has, as its name makes clear, a focus on users – in this case, users of the information system. This follows on from user involvement in the original needs analysis, with an emphasis on continuous involvement and regular communication. This helps to give a sense of ownership to stakeholders, which can assist in people's acceptance of change. As the focus of this book has been on user-centred design, some form of user-centred evaluation is assumed to be essential.

In experimental evaluation objectivity is a key concern. This approach is essentially quantitative and will typically involve conducting small-scale testing in controlled conditions, the outcome of which can be used for generalisation. This is one of the approaches used in the research described in Chapter 2 on picture retrieval strategies. A problem is in reproducing real-world experiences in experimental conditions. It is suggested that experimental evaluation, while being a very useful tool for testing prototypes and system functionality, has to be conducted alongside other evaluation methods.

Responsive evaluation is essentially qualitative. Typically, responsive evaluation will involve observation in real settings so is the opposite of the experimental approach. This type of naturalistic research is time-consuming but will allow for description and analysis of how a system is actually being used in people's working lives.

These various approaches have one factor in common: the desire to provide meaningful information that will help in assessing and enhancing the information architecture. They are also very different in that they cover the whole spectrum of research from the 'scientific' to the 'unscientific'. Ideally a combination of approaches will be used to gather the range of data needed to evaluate the information architecture: from a management perspective, from a user perspective, from a functionality perspective and from a value perspective. In reality there will always be constraints such as limited time, limited resources, organisational politics and organisational culture.

Having looked at evaluation research in the context of the whole information architecture, we will now focus on the information retrieval system. Most evaluation studies in the information sciences concentrate on evaluation criteria for information retrieval systems. Some of this work is highly relevant as it pertains to the efficiency and effectiveness of the search engine and the taxonomy that provide the main retrieval mechanisms of the information system. A lot of effort has gone into solving the problem of how to evaluate information retrieval systems, a lot has been written about systems evaluation, and experiments have been devised to test the quality and value of specific systems and databases. Most of the effort in establishing evaluation criteria has gone into devising quantitative measures of system effectiveness. But it is important to remember that there are both subjective and objective measures of system performance. Subjective measures of system performance, while arguably more important than objective measures, are difficult to test. Because of this, most research into evaluating retrieval systems has been rooted in the scientific approach to investigation that stresses objectivity and the collection of quantifiable data. But even though the following discussion will be concentrating on those scientific, objective measures of system effectiveness, we cannot ignore subjective factors. The ultimate test of system effectiveness is how well it meets the needs of its users, and it is very difficult to measure that in objective terms.

Objective measures of system effectiveness

Support for search and browsing strategies was examined in Chapter 3 and, clearly, the quality of the search facilities and any browsing facilities have to be taken into account when evaluating an information system. The six evaluation criteria that have often been used, that are often examined in the literature and that this section concentrates upon are: recall, precision, effort, time, presentation and coverage. Instead of finding out whether the user is happy or not, instead of finding out about the success of the information retrieval process, these criteria attempt to measure the efficiency of the information retrieval system.

When a user is searching an information system for items on a particular subject, their aim is obviously to retrieve some or all of the items that deal with that subject, and also to not retrieve items that do not deal with that subject: information retrieval is concerned with the selective recovery of items from storage. This leads on to the concepts of recall and precision. Before describing how to calculate recall and precision, the concept of relevance has to be explained. The problem for systems evaluation is that relevance is a subjective notion. Different users might have different views about the relevance or non-relevance of particular items to satisfy particular needs for information. Interestingly, given that they are seen as objective evaluation methods, measuring recall and precision involves judgements of relevance, so there is an element of subjectivity. But, importantly, recall and precision can be expressed in quantitative terms, suggesting a greater level of objectivity than is actually the case. Recall and precision often interact: high recall suggests low precision, high precision suggests low recall.

Recall is the ability of the system to retrieve *all* relevant items. If a user is searching for a particular document, that document is either retrieved from the database – it is recalled – or it is not. If a user is searching for all documents on a particular subject, the success of the search can be said to depend upon the extent to which all the documents on that subject are retrieved. The measure of the completeness of a search is often referred to as the 'recall ratio' – 50 per cent recall means that half of the relevant documents stored in the system were retrieved. Generally, the more broadly defined the search topic, the higher the recall, the greater the number of relevant items retrieved. For example, if someone wanted documents relating to evaluation and testing of information retrieval systems then simply typing the term 'information' in the search box would result in the retrieval of a very high number of relevant records: recall would be high. Of course, the more broadly defined the search topic, the more likely you are to retrieve a high proportion of records that include the key term or terms you input to the system but which are not relevant.

Precision refers to the ability of the system to retrieve *only* the relevant items. A search that retrieves 100 items of which only 10 were judged to be relevant has operated at a precision ratio of 10 per cent. Here the precision ratio is low, but recall may be high – there may not be many relevant items in the system (in which case you know either that not much has been written about that subject or you are searching in the wrong place). A search that retrieves 10 items of which all 10 were judged to be relevant has operated at a precision ratio of 100 per cent. No false drops here, but a lot of potentially relevant documents possibly were not retrieved, so the recall ratio may be low.

As a general rule, the more narrowly defined the search topic, the higher the precision. Everyone should have had experience of this. You might begin a search by typing one or two terms into a search box; then if you do not find what you want, you add more terms or a phrase and perhaps specify fields and limits. In doing so you should have noticed that the number of records retrieved decreased, and hopefully the records you did retrieve increased in relevance – so you were increasing the precision of the search. A perfect search would retrieve all the documents in the system that are judged to be relevant and none that are judged to be non-relevant. In this search the recall ratio would be 100 per cent and the precision ration would be 100 per cent. Someone may, at some point, have conducted a perfect search, but it is something that is certainly outside most people's experience.

Recall and precision can be expressed as simple formulae:

$$\text{Recall} = \frac{\text{Number of relevant documents retrieved}}{\text{Total number of relevant documents in the collection}}$$

$$\text{Precision} = \frac{\text{Number of relevant documents retrieved}}{\text{Total number of documents retrieved}}$$

The outcome of these simple calculations multiplied by 100 will give a percentage value. Together, the recall and precision ratios express the filtering capacity of the retrieval system, its ability to let through what is wanted and to hold back what is not.

Now, as always, you have to consider the needs of the user. Different users may need different levels of recall and precision, or the same user may have different needs at different times. If someone is conducting a comprehensive literature search, they probably want high recall: they do not want to miss anything that is potentially relevant. If someone wants to retrieve a few recent documents on a subject, then they will probably want high precision. In practice, most people settle for a compromise: reasonable recall and a reasonable level of precision.

Levels of recall and precision depend upon the availability of search features and the provision of a taxonomy – where an item's inclusion within a category should guarantee its relevance. Dialog's powerful search tools and the fact that search activity is usually concentrated within narrowly defined parameters (a limited number of databases with specific subject coverage) mean that searches of high precision can be achieved. This was always vital in commercial systems like Dialog where any records retrieved have to be paid for. On the other hand, anyone using a search engine to retrieve information from the web will probably have found that recall seems to be high and that precision seems to be correspondingly low. Very often it seems that no matter how many search terms are combined in a search statement the search engine will still retrieve thousands of documents. That is partly because the store of information being searched is so vast. However, search engines like Google help to increase precision in that they rank documents. Different search engines apply different criteria in relevance ranking of results. Google,[1] for example, uses link popularity as part of its formula to boost the relevance ranking of websites. All search engines, although generally not wanting to provide specific information about how they rank results, will use some form of term frequency and location algorithm: any documents which contain multiple occurrences of all the key terms, closely grouped, and in the URL, tile or first paragraph, will appear at or near the top of the list of results.[2] So discounting any sponsored links, the first few documents in the list of retrieved web pages should be highly relevant.

It should be possible to use recall and precision to test the efficiency of retrieval software in a more controlled environment like an organisation's information system. It should be relatively easy to calculate the precision ratio of a search because it is simply based on the items retrieved (12 items were retrieved, 9 were judged to be relevant by the user: the precision ratio is 75 per cent). It is not so easy to calculate the recall ratio. Remember recall relates to the ability of the system to retrieve all relevant items, so the only way we can work that out is to know beforehand how many relevant items are present in the information store. You conduct a search that retrieves 100 items. Of those 100 items 50 are relevant. The precision ratio is 50 per cent; that is straightforward enough. So what is the recall ratio? The answer is you do not know. It could be 100 per cent: perhaps the 50 relevant items retrieved represent all the relevant items in the database. On the other hand, there might be another 50 items you did not retrieve which are also relevant, in which case recall is 50 per cent. But you do not know that because you have no idea how many relevant items the database contains.

So how can you try to measure recall? One way is to construct the database yourself, so that you know exactly what it contains and then input various search statements to test its ability to retrieve all the relevant items. This was the approach used by early studies into retrieval efficiency like the Cranfield experiments.[3] Another, more practical way to measure recall is to ask several users to search for information on the same topic and to compare their results. The searcher retrieving the highest number of relevant items is assumed to have achieved 100 per cent recall. This type of testing will provide a means of evaluating the retrieval software: any search engine application should be capable of processing user queries, but recall can be increased by the provision of features like word-stemming. Another, more useful way to measure recall is to compare two different applications to obtain a measure of relative recall:

$$\text{Relative recall} = \frac{\text{Number of documents retrieved by application 1}}{\text{Number of documents retrieved by application 2}}$$

So it is possible to compare the performance of two different applications for powering the search engine before deciding which to implement. Comparison is also useful to test for relative precision, by comparing the efficiency of the relevance ranking of two or more applications before deciding which will be implemented.

Recall and precision ratios are the most commonly described evaluation measures in the information management literature. They provide a means of testing search software to increase recall (provision of Boolean OR, word-stemming) and to increase precision (phrase, automatic AND, relevance ranking). But there are other evaluation criteria which are of more obvious concern to the users of an information system: effort, time, presentation and coverage.

Effort relates to the cognitive and physical domains of Kuhlthau's model of the search process.[4] Some types of search strategy use a lot of intellectual effort: for example, formulating a search statement using a controlled vocabulary and Boolean operators. Wandering around the bays as you might do if you are browsing in a library increases physical effort. Exploring a taxonomy to find information should reduce the amount of cognitive or intellectual effort expended but may increase perceived physical effort by requiring multiple mouse clicks. It is certainly true that, from a user's point of view, the less overall effort the better. In the case of a search where the precision ratio is high, the searcher probably used a great deal of intellectual effort in formulating a very precise search statement. In the case of a search where the recall ratio is high, the searcher probably used less effort in formulating the search statement but will have to expend a great deal of effort in looking at all the retrieved documents and selecting those judged most relevant. In measuring effort, you would tend to quantify it in terms of the next criterion, which is time.

Time seems like an obvious one. The shorter the time you have to take to complete the search the better. In a sense, it is that obvious, but you ought to take account of time in terms of both user effort and system response time. If a user is conducting their own search, then effort can be quantified by the amount of time the user spends conducting the search. If an intermediary is conducting the search on behalf of the user, then effort can be measured by the amount of time spent negotiating the enquiry and the amount of time needed to identify relevant items when the search results are delivered. Again this can be related to the precision ratio. If a lot of time and effort are expended in the search formulation or negotiation stage, then the precision ratio should be high and so less time needs to be expended in identifying relevant items. System response time refers to the time it takes to get the results of a search. In this context we can assume it refers to the time the retrieval application takes to process a search and deliver the results. All search engines seem capable of processing searches in a fraction of a second, but it is again useful to compare different applications to test their processing speed. It is also important to bear in mind that this can be affected by the speed of the local network.

Something else that relates to time and effort is the simplicity or user-friendliness of the system. For example, users have to expend a great deal of time and effort in getting to grips with retrieval systems like Dialog. That is because it is not particularly user-friendly, especially in command mode. The system was originally designed to be used by experts – it is not possible to simply sit down and start using the system effectively. In comparison, web search engines are quite user-friendly: the interface makes interaction with the system easy and transparent. Search engines were designed to be used by novice users and require the user to make less expenditure of time and effort in order to learn reasonably effective search skills. Of course, commercial hosts like Dialog deliver results that have already been checked for validity and authority, and the quality of the information itself does not require verification. The time and effort spent in training is more than compensated for by the time and effort saved in checking the information retrieved. In the organisational environment, the quality of the information accessible via the system should be assured through checks in the approval and publication stages of the information life cycle. System features that can improve precision of searching and reduce time and effort were discussed in Chapter 3.

Presentation and coverage are vital and should have been addressed during the information audit and content analysis. Evaluation should show that content is available in forms that users can readily access and make use of: full-text in Word, HTML and PDF, spreadsheets, presentations and so on. Obviously, presentation of the retrieved information is important, but as noted in Chapter 4, the format of the items stored in the system should not actually be an issue if applications are available to read and present the data. Evaluation of coverage should show that all the information the user needs is included in the system.

It is important to note that even if we apply quantitative measures; 'objective' evaluation still includes the user's own subjective evaluation of relevance. It may be better to embrace subjectivity and concentrate evaluation on more user-centred issues – trying to determine whether the user is happy with the system and with the results it provides. Information science has been more concerned with the development of evaluation criteria that can be measured quantitatively, but a mix of quantitative and qualitative methods provides a more effective means of determining the user-centredness of a system.

Evaluating information architectures

So far we have concentrated on evaluation strategies and objective evaluation techniques. We can now use those to develop a more practical framework for evaluation, which also serves as an overview of many of the issues covered in this book. Evaluation can concentrate on four broad areas:

- search and browsing facilities;
- the interface;

- content;
- use and effectiveness.

Search and browsing facilities

Search and browsing facilities were examined in the Chapter 3. A search engine should possess features that will increase the efficiency of search and retrieval and that will accommodate both expert and novice searchers:

Boolean: Default AND to combine search terms
Support for NOT (–) to exclude terms
Support for OR for synonyms and variant spellings
Support for full Boolean searching is desirable but not essential

The default AND and support for the NOT operator increase the precision of searching; support for the OR operator increases recall. Expert searchers will welcome the provision of full Boolean, but this is a feature that is unlikely to be used by the majority of people within the organisation so cannot be regarded as essential.

Phrase: Essential to increase efficiency
Proximity: Desirable but not essential
Truncation: Desirable but not essential
Word stemming: Automatic plurals searching is essential
Fields: Author, title, subject at least
Limits: Date and file type at least

Selecting an application to power the organisation's search engine represents a major decision in the information architecture development process. It is essential that selection is made on the basis of a thorough task analysis and an awareness of user needs. The above criteria can be used in testing and evaluation before a final selection is made.

A taxonomy provides a structure to support browsing activities. The basic principles of taxonomy creation as examined in Chapter 3 can be used in its evaluation. Category names should be clear and unambiguous; terminology should be applied consistently. It is good practice to limit the number of top-level categories – the second level can provide a greater breadth of coverage. Depth of the hierarchy should not exceed five levels. Individual organisational needs will dictate whether a single monohierarchy, multiple hierarchies or a polyhierarchy provides the most effective browsing environment. Subjects should be at a level in the hierarchy that reflects their relationship with other subjects: for example, how broad or how narrow they are. Categories within levels have to be organised in some way and evaluation should involve checking that list ordering within categories is appropriate: logical, sequential or alphabetical.

The interface

Chapter 5 covered the major factors that can be applied in evaluation of the interface. In the context of structure and navigation, consistency of screen layout, provision of permanent objects and visual cues like colour coding can help the user to develop an appropriate mental model of the information space. Visual design is vitally important in promoting positive affect. Is the overall design attractive, and are aesthetic principles adhered to in screen layout and use of graphics and colour? This can help to speed or slow completion of tasks and extraction of information. Have fonts and font sizes been chosen to maximise legibility? Have the needs of users with visual impairment or other disabilities been taken into account?

As well as providing access to documentation, the information architecture has to support information flow across the organisation by providing access to e-mail, e-bulletin boards, news and events information and so on. Have all these interactive elements been incorporated effectively into the overall design?

Content

In Chapter 4 we concentrated upon the content at the heart of the system. Information becomes content when it has been described, structured and organised. Evaluation should seek evidence that coverage is comprehensive and that individual documents have been analysed and described using standard metadata, and their content components identified, mapped and managed. Evaluation should also check that vocabulary control is being exercised in describing content. Identification of equivalence and associative relationships among subjects as seen in thesauri has the potential to greatly increase the efficiency of taxonomies and search engines.

Use and effectiveness

Use and effectiveness is the most difficult evaluation criterion to objectify but is really concerned with fitness for purpose. Does the information architecture achieve the goals stated at the start of the project? This requires an assessment of how far the outcomes of the information audit examined in Chapter 2 have influenced the overall design. Are user needs supported? Are user tasks supported? Are individual differences catered for? Issues that have already been raised in the previous three headings are of obvious relevance here, and these can be assessed with some level of objectivity. A true evaluation of use and effectiveness will, however, involve soliciting user opinion via questionnaires, interviews and focus groups, and will also involve observation to assess actual use of the system. So we have come full circle: the design process began with user research and the post-deployment evaluation requires ongoing user research to monitor the information architecture's continuing effectiveness.

Final thoughts on information architecture development

Rosenfeld and Morville take a very pragmatic approach to managing design and implementation, and point out that no matter how important the concept of information architecture is to the organisation and no matter how great the new system is, there are some people who just will not be interested. You can hope that people will come around to accepting the system and so you should make sure that it meets their needs – that the information they need will be there or can be easily accommodated – but you should not waste too much time with them. Instead you should concentrate on:

- 'killer content' – focus on the people who create or own the really important information;
- the most enthusiastic users – the ones who want change and will give you time and support;

- the users with the most influence and resources – money, technical expertise, etc.[5]

Rosenfeld and Morville also differentiate between strategy and tactics: strategy is top-down, tactics are bottom-up – basically, the managers versus the workers. They suggest that, to try to balance the needs of both, you need two teams: the strategy team and the tactical team, which they call the strategic unit and the operations unit. They describe the strategic unit as being like a board of directors (in fact it may be the board of directors). Its purpose is really to devise the strategy and policy we looked at earlier.

The operations team does the tactical work: the research, the design, the deployment. Rosenfeld and Morville define some of the roles that members of the operations team would have to perform and identify how it should be staffed:

- strategy architect
- thesaurus designer
- interaction architect
- technology integration specialist
- information architecture usability specialist
- search analyst
- controlled vocabulary manager
- indexing specialist
- content modelling architect
- ethnographer
- project manager.[6]

Some of these roles may, of course, overlap. The thesaurus designer, controlled vocabulary manager and the indexing specialist may be the same person. This effectively and concisely demonstrates the scope of information architecture.

Final thoughts on information architects

It was stated in the introductory chapter that information professionals already, to a greater or lesser extent, 'do' information architecture. There are so many different roles and job titles associated with information architecture that a definition of an information architect is as unclear as the definitions of the subject area. A recent study by Dooley[7] attempts to discover how information architects define themselves. The results are interesting in that they demonstrate the breadth of the field and many areas of overlap with traditional librarianship.

Dooley found that those people she surveyed with the title of Information Architect tended to focus on content management, metadata creation and checking – in fact their role was very similar to that of a cataloguer in the traditional library environment. Her results indicated that most people working in information architecture tended to specialise in one aspect of the field – as suggested by their job titles (see Figure 7.1).

It is interesting to note that many of the key skills mentioned by people working in information architecture are generic rather than subject-specific (see Figure 7.2). As Dooley points out, if you can deal in detail with large and complex information problems, find solutions and communicate these effectively then you have many of the skills necessary to be an information architect.

Figure 7.1 Information architect: job titles

Designer

Experience Architect

Head of Development

Head of User Experience

Information Architect

Interaction Designer

Interactive & CRM Manager

Interface Designer

Language Specialist/Terminologist

Usability Engineer

User Experience Architect

Web Developer

Figure 7.2	Information architecture: skills

Top three key skills:

Ability to see patterns/solutions

Attention to detail

Communication skills

Other key skills:

Broad knowledge

Design skills

Good listener

Influencing/persuading skills

Innovation

IT literacy to high level

Language skills

Logic

Organisational ability

Patience

People skills

Presentation skills

Project management

Team player

User research techniques

References

1. Google: *http://www.google.com/corporate/tech.html* (accessed 29 August 2006).
2. Monash, C.A. *Search Engine Ranking Algorithms,* available at: *http://www.monash.com/search_engine_ranking.html* (accessed 29 August 2006).
3. Cleverdon, C.W. et al. (1966) *Factors Determining the Performance of Indexing Systems.* Cranfield: Aslib Cranfield Research Project.

4. Kuhlthau, C.C. (1994) *Seeking Meaning: A Process Approach to Library and Information Services*. Norwood, NJ: Ablex.

5. Rosenfeld, L. and Morville, P. (2002) *Information Architecture for the World Wide Web*, 2nd edn. Sebastopol, CA: O'Reilly, p. 372.

6. Ibid., p. 378.

7. Dooley, H. (2006) 'Media Darlings: How Far Do Information Architects Working in UK Media Organisations Stray from the Notion of the Traditional Librarian?' Unpublished MA dissertation, London Metropolitan University, p. 194.

Appendix 1
Dewey Decimal Schedules: extract

Here is part of the Dewey Decimal Schedules for regional medicine. The listing in the schedules is more detailed – only the listing for abdominal and pelvic cavities at 617.55 is presented in detail:

617.51 Head

617.52 Face

617.53 Neck

617.54 Thorax (Chest) and respiratory system

617.55 Abdominal and pelvic cavities

      617.551 Spleen

      617.553 Stomach (including pylorus)

      617.554 Intestine

            617.5541 Small intestine (including duodenum, jejunum, ileum)

            617.5545 Cecum, vermiform appendix

            617.5547 Large intestine (including sigmoid colon)

      617.555 Rectum, anus, perineum

      617.556 Biliary tract and liver

            617.5562 Liver

            617.5565 Gallbladder

            617.5567 Bile ducts

      617.557 Pancreas and islands of Langerhans

      617.558 Peritoneum (including mesentery, omentum)

      617.559 Hernias (including hiatal hernia)

617.56 Back

617.57 Upper extremities

617.58 Lower extremities

Appendix 2
Alphabetical listing

Abdominal and pelvic cavities

Anus

Back

Bile ducts

Biliary tract and liver

Cecum

Chest USE Thorax

Colon USE Large intestine

Duodenum USE Small intestine

Face

Gallbladder

Head

Hernias

Hiatal hernia USE Hernias

Ileum USE Small intestine

Inguinal hernia USE Hernias

Intestine

Jejunum USE Small intestine

Large intestine

Liver

Lower extremities

Mesentery USE Peritoneum

Neck

Omentum USE Peritoneum

Pancreas and islands of Langerhans
Perineum
Peritoneum
Pylorus USE Stomach
Rectum
Sigmoid colon USE Large intestine
Small intestine
Spleen
Stomach
Thorax and respiratory system
Upper extremities
Vermiform appendix

Appendix 3
Thesaurus entries

Abdominal and pelvic cavities
	BT	Regional medicine
	NT	Intestine
		Spleen
		Stomach
	RT	Back
		Thorax and respiratory system

Anus
	BT	Abdominal and pelvic cavities
	RT	Peritoneum
		Rectum

Back
	BT	Regional medicine
	RT	Abdominal and pelvic cavities
		Lower extremities
		Upper extremities

Bile ducts
	BT	Biliary tract and liver
	RT	Gallbladder
		Liver

Biliary tract and liver
	BT	Abdominal and pelvic cavities
	NT	Bile ducts
		Gallbladder
		Liver

	RT	Anus
		Hernias
		Intestine
		Pancreas and islands of Langerhans
Cecum		
	BT	Intestine
	RT	Large intestine
		Small intestine
		Vermiform appendix

Chest USE Thorax

Colon USE Large intestine

Duodenum USE Small intestine

Face		
	BT	Regional medicine
	RT	Head
		Neck
Gallbladder		
	BT	Biliary tract and liver
	RT	Bile ducts
		Liver
Head		
	BT	Regional medicine
	RT	Face
		Neck
Hernias		
	UF	Hiatal hernia
		Inguinal hernia
	BT	Abdominal and pelvic cavities
	RT	Anus
		Biliary tract and liver
		Intestine
		Pancreas and islands of Langerhans
		Perineum

Peritoneum

Rectum

Spleen

Stomach

Hiatal hernia USE Hernias

Ileum USE Small intestine

Inguinal hernia USE Hernias

Intestine

	BT	Abdominal and pelvic cavities
	NT	Cecum
		Large intestine
		Small intestine
		Vermiform appendix
	RT	Anus
		Biliary tract and liver
		Hernias
		Pancreas and islands of Langerhans
		Perineum
		Peritoneum
		Rectum
		Spleen
		Stomach

Jejunum USE Small intestine

Large intestine

	UF	Colon
		Sigmoid colon
	BT	Intestine
	RT	Cecum
		Small intestine
		Vermiform appendix

Liver

	BT	Biliary tract and liver
	RT	Bile ducts
		Gallbladder

Lower extremities
        BT   Regional medicine
        RT   Back
                Upper extremities

Mesentery USE Peritoneum

Neck
        BT   Regional medicine
        RT   Back
                Face
                Head
                Thorax and respiratory system

Omentum USE Peritoneum

Pancreas and islands of Langerhans
        BT   Abdominal and pelvic cavities
        RT   Anus
                Biliary tract and liver
                Hernias
                Intestine
                Perineum
                Peritoneum
                Rectum
                Spleen
                Stomach

Perineum
        BT   Abdominal and pelvic cavities
        RT   Anus
                Biliary tract and liver
                Hernias
                Intestine
                Pancreas and islands of Langerhans
                Peritoneum
                Rectum
                Spleen
                Stomach

Peritoneum
UF Mesentery
Omentum
BT Abdominal and pelvic cavities
RT Anus
Biliary tract and liver
Hernias
Intestine
Pancreas and islands of Langerhans
Perineum
Rectum
Spleen
Stomach
Pylorus USE Stomach
Rectum
BT Abdominal and pelvic cavities
RT Anus
Biliary tract and liver
Hernias
Intestine
Pancreas and islands of Langerhans
Perineum
Peritoneum
Spleen
Stomach
Sigmoid colon USE Large intestine
Small intestine
UF Duodenum
Ileum
Jejunum
BT Abdominal and pelvic cavities
RT Cecum
Large intestine
Vermiform appendix

Spleen
     BT   Abdominal and pelvic cavities
     RT   Anus
              Biliary tract and liver
              Hernias
              Intestine
              Pancreas and islands of Langerhans
              Perineum
              Peritoneum
              Rectum
              Stomach
Stomach
     UF   Pylorus
     BT   Abdominal and pelvic cavities
     RT   Anus
              Biliary tract and liver
              Hernias
              Intestine
              Pancreas and islands of Langerhans
              Perineum
              Peritoneum
              Rectum
              Spleen
Thorax and respiratory system
     UF   Chest
     BT   Regional medicine
     RT   Abdominal and pelvic cavities
              Back
              Head
              Neck
Upper extremities
     BT   Regional medicine
     RT   Back
              Lower extremities
              Thorax and respiratory system

Vermiform appendix
> BT   Abdominal and pelvic cavities
> RT   Cecum
>   Large intestine
>   Small intestine

Appendix 4
Term tree

Medicine
    Regional medicine
        Abdominal and pelvic cavities
            Anus
            Biliary tract and liver
                Bile ducts
                Gallbladder
                Liver
            Hernias
            Intestine
                Cecum
                Large intestine
                Small intestine
                Vermiform appendix
            Pancreas and islands of Langerhans
            Perineum
            Peritoneum
            Rectum
            Spleen
            Stomach
        Back
        Face
        Head
        Lower extremities
        Neck
        Thorax and respiratory system
        Upper extremities

Index

aesthetics, 136
affordances, 133–4
alphabetical indexes, 4
Alta Vista, 58, 130
Amazon, 36–8
analytical strategies, 50–1
Anglo-American Cataloguing Rules, 9
anomalous states of knowledge, 20
architecture:
  definition, 2
archiving, 170–1
artificial intelligence, 124
Ask, 130
ASSIA Thesaurus, 109
associative links, 149
associative relationships, 5, 112, 189
automatic indexing, 101

BBC, 139
berrypicking, 50
Bliss Bibliographic Classification,
  71–2, 83
Bluesheets, 63
bookmarks, 151
Boolean operators, 5, 56–8, 66,
  185–6, 188
breadcrumbs, 149–51
British Library, 139, 151
browsing, 42–3, 49, 51–2, 67, 73–4,
  86, 188
building-blocks, 51

cataloguing, 3, 8–9, 106, 175
classic thesaurus, 54, 114–15
classification, 3, 5–8, 67–74
classified indexes, 5
closed questions, 24
cognitive psychology, 123
cognitive science, 124
cognitive styles, 35–6
collocation, 71
colour-coding, 151, 154, 189
commands, 127
communication channels, 21–3, 173
computational linguistics, 124
concept maps, 16
consistency, 135–7
constraints, 134
content:
  components, 97–100
  definition, 83
  gathering, 96
  mapping, 96–100
  page, 139
content management policy, 171–2
content management systems, 3,
  168
coordinate indexes, 4–5, 50
coverage, 187
Cranfield, 185

descriptor groups, 114
device-dependent tasks, 28–9, 31–2

Dewey Decimal Classification, 49, 67–70, 73–4, 80, 88, 112
Dialog, 58, 62–6, 102, 125, 127, 184, 187
direct manipulation, 130, 133

effort, 185
e-Government Metadata Standard, 103
enumerative classification, 67–70, 73, 82
Epicurious, 144
equivalence relationships, 5, 112–13, 115, 189
ergonomics, 123
ERIC Thesaurus, 109, 113–14
evaluation research, 179–80
Exalead, 58, 62
excluders, 43–4
Expedia, 130
experimental evaluation, 180–1
expert users, 39, 127
explorers, 44
expressiveness, 67–71, 73, 80–1
extranets, 122, 157, 176

faceted classification, 67–8, 70–2, 82, 116
feedback, 134–5
field dependence, 35
field independence, 35
fields, 63–6, 102, 208
findability, 3
Firefox, 151
focusers, 43–4
fonts, 157, 189
forgiveness, 136
form filling, 130

generic tasks, 28, 31
global navigation, 139, 151

goal-oriented evaluation, 180
golden section, 138–9
GOMS model, 39
Google, 5, 58, 62–3, 80, 125, 130, 154, 184
gradation by speciality, 72
Guardian, 144
gulfs of execution and evaluation, 133

helpful order, 72–3
hierarchical relationships, 112
hierarchies, 52, 67–70, 74, 76, 80–1
high-level content, 94–5, 194
holists, 35
home page, 139, 144
hospitality, 67–71, 73, 80
Hotbot, 160
HTML, 103
human factors, 123
human-computer interaction, 9, 27, 122–4
human-information interaction, 122
hypertexts, 144

icons, 126–7, 135
indexes, 4
indexing, 3–4, 76
indexing thesaurus, 114
individual:
    differences, 34–6, 44, 67, 190
    knowledge, 33
    resources, 3, 14
inference rules, 115–16
information:
    chunks, 97–100, 176
    definition, 1
    flows, 17, 21–3, 26, 172, 189
    gaps, 17
    life-cycle, 168–9, 173
    maps, 14–16
    tasks, 3, 13, 28–31

Inspec Thesaurus, 109, 113
interaction models, 125
intermediate navigation page, 139
Internet Explorer, 126, 135, 144, 151
interoperability, 103
interviews, 24–7, 190
intranets, 122, 154, 157, 176
intuitiveness, 135

keyword searching, 42–3, 50–1, 74, 76
knowledge architecture, 3
knowledge assets, 17
knowledge management, 16–17, 26
knowledgeable intermittent users, 39, 127
Kuhlthau's model, 30–1, 44, 49–50, 121, 185

library classification, 6–8, 67–73, 80, 88
Library of Congress:
  Classification, 68–9
  Subject Headings, 107
limits, 63–6, 102, 208

mappings, 134
MARC21, 9, 102–4
Medical Subject Headings, 109
mental maps, 151
menus, 127, 130
metadata:
  definition, 101
Microsoft Word, 126
monohierarchies, 82–3, 86

natural language, 130
needs analysis, 13
Noah's Ark, 96
Northern Light, 62
novice users, 39, 127, 187

observation, 24–6, 40–1, 190
Occam's razor, 135
OCLC, 81, 104
ontology:
  definition, 115
Open Directory, 5, 74–6, 80–1, 83, 149, 151
open questions, 25
organisational culture, 34
organisational knowledge, 34
organisational needs, 16, 21–3, 189

page layout, 138, 189
pearl-growing, 51
permanent objects, 139, 151, 189
personas, 40, 42
phrase searching, 58, 66, 208
picture asymmetry, 138
polyhierarchies, 82–3, 86
post-coordination, 5, 50, 107
precision, 182–5
pre-coordination, 5, 80, 107
preferred terms, 4
presentation, 187
prevention, 136
principle of least effort, 135
procedural knowledge, 33–4
proximity searching, 58, 62, 66, 208

qualitative research, 23, 25–7, 43, 181, 207
quantitative research, 23–7, 43, 180, 207
questionnaires, 24–7, 190

recall, 182–5
records:
  form, 95–6, 98, 195
  function, 95, 98, 195
  management, 8, 94–5, 98, 195
  status, 95, 98, 195

referencing, 5, 107–8
relevance, 182
relevance ranking, 184
representative documents, 96–7
representative tasks, 32, 41–2
resource description, 101, 103
responsive evaluation, 180–1
rights' management, 103

search engines, 49–51, 53–7, 101–2, 184, 186–8
search logic, 56–8
search tactics, 30, 35, 42, 49–50, 53, 67
search terms, 54–6
searching thesaurus, 114
Sears List of Subject Headings, 107–8
semantic knowledge, 33–4
serialists, 35
simplicity, 135, 137, 186
site maps, 149
software engineering, 123
Stanford Web Credibility Project, 121–2
Star user interface, 125
structural navigation links, 144
sub-tasks, 28
subject analysis, 86
subject headings lists, 107
subject trees, 5, 67, 76, 81–3
subordination, 71–2

synonyms, 4
system models, 125

task decomposition, 32
term trees, 113
thesauri, 54, 83
Thesaurus of Psychological Index Terms, 109
time, 186
truncation, 62, 66, 208

Universal Decimal Classification, 71
user-centred design, 3, 9–10, 125
user-oriented evaluation, 180
users, 13, 39, 127

visual impairment, 161, 189
vocabulary control, 4, 54, 76, 80, 82, 87–8, 107, 186, 189

wanderers, 44
web directories, 74–82
Webby awards, 144, 154, 162–3
WIMP, 125, 130
word form, 87, 108, 111
word stemming, 62, 66, 74, 208

Xerox, 125
XML, 103

Yahoo, 5, 80–1, 154

Printed in the United States
108918LV00001B/81/A

9 781843 342328